UNITED

CARLING
PREMIERSHIP

RLING

MPIONS

£5.25

PFA PLAYER OF THE YEAR 1996

Les Ferdinand

NEWCASTLE

STORY OF THE SEASON

AUGUST

JUST three months after Blackburn and Manchester United went to the wire in pursuit of the title, Premiership football was back and here's SHOOT's review of how the title chase went to the last kick for the second successive year...

Jurgen Klinsmann may have gone after being crowned Footballer of the Year but otherwise Europe's finest were flocking to England.

Arsenal lined up with David Platt and Dennis Bergkamp in partnership, David Ginola was geeing up the Geordies, Ruud Gullit let his hair down at Chelsea while hot shot Tony Yeboah and Eric Cantona had pledged to stay at Elland Road and Old Trafford.

Normal service was resumed elsewhere. The opening day of the season saw goals for Alan Shearer, £8.5m man Stan Collymore, the Toon Army's new hero Les Ferdinand and Teddy Sheringham. Matt Le Tissier hit three - but the Saints were marched on by Forest.

Title favourites Manchester United slip up 3-1 at Aston Villa in their first match and questions are asked over the wisdom of selling Paul Ince, Mark Hughes and Andrei Kanchelskis. Even Villa boss Brian Little says: "I thought they would be better than that."

But Alex Ferguson's boys respond like Champions by winning their next five. The write-offs are right up there!

Ray Harford must have been begging for Kenny Dalglish to come down from the directors' box as

Champs Blackburn lose three of their first four games.

The people's favourites, Newcastle, hit the heights as Kevin Keegan's side win their first four. Yeboah meanwhile stakes an early claim for Goal of the Season with a missile against Liverpool.

Hot-headed Irish star Roy Keane gets his first sight of the red card. He is sent-off in Manchester United's 2-1 win at Blackburn after diving in the box.

Newly-promoted Middlesbrough move into the state-of-the-art £16m Riverside Stadium and baptise it with a 2-0 win at home to Chelsea.

STORY OF THE SEASON

SEPTEMBER

Tony Yeboah is at it again. He hits three in a 4-2 demolition of Wimbledon including a stunning solo effort which almost busts the goal.

Robbie Fowler gives Terry Venables a timely nudge with four out of Liverpool's five against Bolton. Andy Cole, on the other hand, spends September on the sidelines through injury.

Alan Shearer registers his first hat-trick of the season, against Coventry, while Ruud Gullit and Dennis Bergkamp open their accounts.

Jason McAteer is the latest recruit to Roy Evans' Anfield revolution. Bolton's Republic of Ireland man signs

Sharpe. Boss Joe Royle rues: "Unbelievable - tackling is not in Anders contract." The Russian flier joins Duncan Ferguson on the long-term casualty list.

Manchester City end the month rock bottom after a 3-0 mauling at Nottingham Forest. Just one point and three goals in eight games puts Alan Ball's future in jeopardy. Meanwhile, across the city, l'enfant terrible is waiting in the wings...

on the dotted line for £4.5m - and blames Kenny Dalglish for the move! "It's his fault that I'm so passionate about Liverpool," says Macca.

Newcastle suffer their first hiccup, a 1-0 defeat at Southampton where Jim Magilton is on target. Manchester United take the opportunity to join Keegan's team at the top after a 3-2 win at Everton. But the game is marred by an injury to Andrei Kanchelskis against his former club. He dislocates a shoulder after coming off worse in a challenge with Lee

OCTOBER

Eight months after going over the top (of the perimeter boards) at Selhurst Park, Eric Cantona is back.

Never has one man's suspension so caught the imagination and Old Trafford gleefully hails the saviour's return. And the scriptwriters add to the fun by ensuring his comeback match is at home to United's bitter foe Liverpool.

The T-shirts proclaimed: "He's been punished for his mistakes ... Now it's someone else's turn!" And not even Liverpool are allowed to gatecrash the party. The visitors go 2-1 up but with time running out United are awarded a penalty. Up steps Cantona, as cool as you like, to stroke in the equaliser. Cue, bedlam.

The chaos at Old Trafford cannot interrupt Newcastle's serene start to the campaign. Les Ferdinand makes it 13 in 10 League games with one on his return to Loftus Road followed by a hat-trick in a 6-1 demolition of Wimbledon.

Vinnie Jones was firmly in the firing line as he took the gloves from Paul Heald after the 'keeper's dismissal.

Keegan promptly demands an England place for big Les after he is left out of the trip to Norway. "He spent all last week answering questions on why he wasn't in the England side," says Keegan. "He has spent the last two Saturdays showing why he should be."

The transfer market hots up again. Ruel Fox moves from Newcastle to Spurs for £4.2m, Sheffield Wednesday splash out £4m on Belgrade boys Darko Kovacevic and Dejan Stefanovic while the prince of Samba arrives on Teesside. Bryan Robson shells out £4.75m for pint-sized wonderboy Juninho but a snag with work permits delays his debut for a month.

The Maine Road crisis gathers pace after a 6-0 mauling at Anfield. Manchester City look doomed after taking just two points from a possible 33.

NOVEMBER

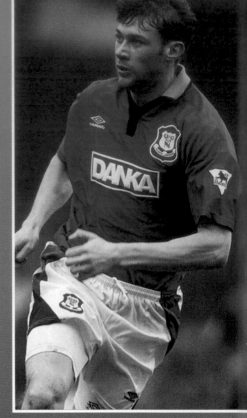

For the second successive year, the chase for the Premiership is resembling a two-horse race. Liverpool hand the initiative to Manchester United and Newcastle after claiming a solitary point from four matches over the month. Newcastle are three points clear after beating Leeds 2-1.

Chelsea chairman Ken Bates bans club owner Matthew Harding from the directors' box as the war for control of Stamford Bridge gathers steam.

Swedish superstar Tomas Brolin becomes the latest import as he joins Leeds from Italian giants Parma. Arsenal and Newcastle go shopping for Paul Ince but the England midfielder opts to stay with Inter Milan.

Everton's Duncan Ferguson is released from prison where he had served three months for assault - and is told he must miss the next 12 games. The Scottish FA had imposed the ban but a judicial review backs 'Duncan Disorderly' and he's allowed to return immediately.

Back on the pitch, Alan Shearer shows what he can't do for England he manages at Blackburn. Another Shearer hat-trick sets up Rovers for a 7-0 humbling of Forest.

Bolton go bottom after three more defeats while Alan Ball's strugglers suddenly get the winning habit.

QPR, Sheffield Wednesday and Wimbledon announce their relegation credentials by going through the month without a win. The Dons' 4-1 loss at Forest was their seventh straight defeat and they had Vinnie Jones sent-off for good measure.

DECEMBER

Feuding Chelsea chiefs Ken Bates and Matthew Harding declare a truce and sit side by side in the directors' box as the Blues beat Newcastle 1-0.

Graeme Le Saux is resigned to missing the European Championship after sustaining a broken leg in Blackburn's 1-0 win against Middlesbrough. Le Saux's club are also the biggest movers in the transfer market by signing Chris Coleman from Crystal Palace for £2.8m while £2m Noel Whelan quits Leeds for Coventry.

Vinnie Jones is in trouble again with one of his legendary acts of diplomacy. Sent-off for a lunge at Ruud Gullit, the Dons iron man makes matters worse by attacking the Dutch legend in a national newspaper. He likened Gullit to two pot-bellied pigs he owns but adds: "They don't squeal as much as him." Inevitably, the result is a trip to the FA to face a disrepute charge.

Savo Milosevic grabs his first hat-trick for Aston Villa in a 4-1 victory over Coventry. Hat-tricks are also netted by Blackburn's Alan Shearer (4-2 v West Ham) Liverpool terror Robbie Fowler (3-1 v Arsenal) and Dion Dublin whose efforts counted for nothing, Sheffield Wednesday beating Coventry 4-3.

Manchester United suffer two reverses in a week to upset their Championship chase. Robbie Fowler scores both goals in a 2-0 loss at Liverpool which is followed by a 3-1 defeat at Leeds. But Newcastle aren't having it all their own way. Defeat at Stamford Bridge preceded a 2-0 choker at Old Trafford in the biggest game of the season. Andy Cole may be having a poor season but he takes great pleasure in putting one over his former club.

Bolton have become marooned at the foot of the table and go into the New Year without a win in their previous 10 games. Christmas is here and we still haven't seen a manager sacked. Yet!

STORY OF THE SEASON

JANUARY

The first managerial casualty arrives and, surprise, surprise, it's Bolton's Roy McFarland who gets the brown envelope. A 4-2 loss at Sheffield Wednesday to kick off the New Year signalled the end, leaving his partner Colin Todd in sole command. Todd begins with a 1-0 win against Wimbledon.

Cup exits at the hands of Chelsea and Arsenal only serve to tighten Newcastle's grip on the Premiership. January offers up three games, three wins against Arsenal, Coventry and Bolton.

Manchester United's challenge appears to be fading after a 4-1 thumping at White Hart Lane and a goalless draw at home to Aston Villa. By the end of the month, Newcastle are 12 points clear. But it's Liverpool in second place thanks to the best partnership in the land, Stan Collymore and Robbie Fowler.

Upton Park, once the `Academy of Football' but now the `League of Nations', welcomes two more foreigners - Ilie Dumitrescu and Slaven Bilic. Two former England internationals on the move are Andy Sinton (Sheff Wed to Spurs) and Nigel Clough (Liverpool to Man City).

QPR and Boro go through the month without a win to enter the relegation dogfight. Terry Venables announces his retirement from the England job after Euro 96. Just about every manager in the Premiership is tipped to replace him. Second prize is succeeding Jack Charlton who quits the Republic of Ireland.

STORY OF THE SEASON

FEBRUARY

Kevin Keegan splashes out twice more, investing more than £10m in Faustino Asprilla and David Batty.

Colombian striker Asprilla's on-off transfer is finally resolved with the ex-Parma man saying: "I feel like a doll that has been tossed about." Asprilla comes off the bench on his debut to set up Steve Watson in a 2-1 win at Middlesbrough.

Asprilla then scores against Manchester City but is twice involved in clashes with Keith Curle, the second a head-butt after the final whistle.

Newcastle are also beaten at West Ham and Manchester United take the chance to cut the deficit. Four wins in February culminating in a 6-0 hammering of Bolton resurrect their hopes.

Earlier devil-turned-saint, Eric Cantona, returned to Selhurst Park, the scene of his infamous kung-fu assault 12 months earlier, and was crowned with two goals in a 4-2 defeat of Wimbledon.

And Liverpool's win at Blackburn keeps them in the hunt.

Coventry's Ron Atkinson is the month's

other big spender with £2m to Aberdeen for Eoin Jess and £1.5m to Birmingham for Liam Daish.

Not to be outdone by their Tyneside rivals, Middlesbrough go shopping again and come up with Brazilian midfielder Branco and a 0-0 draw at Coventry ends a run of eight straight defeats for Boro..

Alan Shearer bags yet another hat-trick, this time against luckless Bolton who remain rooted to the foot of the table, five points adrift of QPR.

STORY OF THE SEASON

MARCH

March begins with the Championship showdown between Newcastle and Manchester United at fortress St James.

Thirteen wins out of 13 at home made the Geordies favourites but it counted for nothing. Peter Schmeichel produced the early heroics and Eric Cantona the second-half goal as the Red Devils escaped with the spoils.

Transfer deadline day is preceded by Ian Wright slapping in a transfer request to Bruce Rioch. Arsenal's directors reject it out of hand but Chelsea boss Glenn Hoddle stays alert.

Blackburn snap up Manchester City's Garry Flitcroft for £3.2m - and he is sent-off on his debut at home to Everton - after three minutes! City, in turn, buy Russian Mikhael Kavelashvili while Wednesday also look overseas for Feyenoord's Regi Blinker.

The month is all about Eric Cantona as Manchester United close in on shaky Newcastle.

The wayward Frenchman who has suddenly become Old Trafford's calming influence, scores an injury time equaliser at Loftus Road, a stunner to beat Arsenal and the only goal at home to Tottenham.

Up in the North-East, Newcastle hammer 10-man West Ham but come unstuck at Arsenal. Fergie's side are back on top of the Premiership. Liverpool keep up their momentum with victories against Villa and Chelsea but defeat at Forest does them no favours.

Alan Shearer gets yet another hat-trick at Tottenham while wins against Leeds, Coventry and Sheffield Wednesday give Bolton a lifeline.

STORY OF THE SEASON

APRIL

April starts with the match of the season and ends with Kevin Keegan (below) losing his rag in front of millions on TV.

A tense month kicks off with a spell-binding seven goal thriller at Anfield. Liverpool's and Newcastle's defences go walkabout and the goals flow. Newcastle go 3-2 up but Stan Collymore has the last laugh with an injury time winner (below).

A week later: Another disaster. David Batty's first goal for the club - against former team Blackburn - puts Keegan's stars in charge, but Geordie boy Graham Fenton comes off the bench to score twice in the last four minutes and shatter the title dream.

Manchester United are now in the box seat. Wins at Maine Road, and at home to Coventry, put them six points clear but, inevitably, nothing is clear cut. Just as Fergie can see the Premiership trophy heading back to Old Trafford they crash 3-1 at Southampton.

Now, Manchester United have three games left, Newcastle five and if they are all wins, the title will be decided on goal difference.

And so it happens...Newcastle edge out Aston Villa and Southampton while United squeeze past Leeds. They then crush Nottingham Forest 5-0 to seize the goalscoring initiative, before Newcastle's visit to Elland Road and victory courtesy

of Keith Gillespie's rare header. And then Keegan flips.

Fergie's sly digs over the past few weeks could have been brushed off. But keegan roars back: "A lot of things have been said. A lot of it slanderous. Alex Ferguson has gone down in my estimation. I will love it if we beat them to the title. Love it."

Bolton and QPR go down, but Southampton, Coventry and Manchester City, level on points above them, take the race for the third relegation place into the final week after victories in their penultimate games.

Coventry's David Busst (below) and Villa's Gary Charles suffer sickening leg injuries. Busst's shattered leg, which held up play at Old Trafford for 15 minutes, has put the 29-year old defender's career under threat.

Eric Cantona causes a stir by seeing off Chelsea's Ruud Gullit for the Football Writers' Association Footballer of the Year award.

MAY

After a season of many twists and turns, Manchester United (right) kill the drama at the Riverside Stadium to clinch their third Premier League title in four years.

Alex Ferguson's side needed only a point at Middlesbrough to win their 10th Championship. An early goal by David May ensured there would be no final slip up, and second-half strikes from Andy Cole and Ryan Giggs put the issue beyond doubt.

Newcastle's 1-1 draw at Nottingham Forest 72 hours earlier had effectively ended the title race. The Geordies finished their campaign with another draw against Spurs but were cheered by the news that manager Kevin Keegan would stay at least another season at St James' Park.

Tears of joy at Old Trafford were matched by tears of sorrow across Manchester at Maine Road. Manchester City (below) fell victim to the Alan Ball curse and were relegated, despite a 2-2 draw against Liverpool.

Coventry and Southampton both earned scoreless draws to avoid the drop on goal difference. City became the fifth Alan Ball side to be relegated in the former World Cup winner's management career.

A late goal by Dennis Bergkamp earned Arsenal a 2-1 win against Bolton and a UEFA Cup spot. Until the Dutchman scored in the 86th minute at Highbury, Spurs, Blackburn and, most particularly, Everton were still in the running for Europe.

The FA announce that Chelsea manager Glenn Hoddle (right) will become the ninth man to take charge of the England national team, in succession to Terry Venables. The official job title is England coach, not manager, and Hoddle will begin his duties in earnest after the European Championship. FA Chief Executive Graham Kelly said Hoddle was appointed because he "shared the same philosophies" as Venables - and because he groomed Michael Duberry from the Chelsea youth team all the way to first-team level.

Trust Eric Cantona to complete Manchester United's miraculous season. Old Trafford leaps into the history books with the first Double-Double - Champions and, icing on the cake, FA Cup winners for a record ninth time. Cantona's winning Wembley goal over Liverpool, four minutes from time, was enough to make Alex Ferguson throw away his chewing gum!

Ruud Gullit is appointed player-manager of Chelsea - then finds that chairman Ken Bates and director Matthew Harding are locked in yet another Stamford Bridge boardroom battle. Gullit says: "I don't know what they are fighting about." And so say all of us!

Super Strikers

SHOOT puts the spotlight on the country's top strikers - the players who make life a misery for defenders throughout the land. You'll find all the best in this super section with interviews and posters of Blackburn and England's Alan Shearer, Liverpool's Robbie Fowler, Villa's Dwight Yorke, Celtic's Van Hooydonk, Tottenham's Teddy Sheringham and Manchester United's superstar Ryan Giggs...

Alan Shearer

Q: IS IT IMPORTANT TO WORK HARD AT YOUR GAME?
Alan: It has been part of my game to work hard ever since I started playing and I suppose that must be the first rule of any player, whether their job is to score goals or stop them. You have to work hard at your particular skills, but also have to work hard for general fitness and basic football abilities that are necessary for any player.

Q: DID YOU HAVE A SPECIAL COACH WHEN YOU WERE A YOUNGSTER?
Alan: When I was a lad, my father used to coach me and he would keep me working hard at shooting, passing, heading and everything else. And I used to find a wall to practice against on my own.

Q: WHO WERE YOUR HEROES?
Alan: My heroes were Pele and Gary Lineker. I used to watch them on TV and video as much as possible.

You can pick up a lot from watching other people, especially if they make a mistake and you can see why.

Q: ARE YOU HAPPY TO KEEP TAKING THE HEADLINES AT ROVERS?
Alan: I've always said that however many goals I score they are all attributable to the rest of the team because someone who is an out and out striker is only as good as the other players who are feeding him the opportunities. But you have to play your part as well, of course.

Q: IS IT IMPORTANT TO HAVE GOOD SERVICE?
Alan: I thrive on it and without it I wouldn't score. Chances come in all kinds of ways from crosses, passes and others. That is why it is important to practice heading, volleying, shooting and simple tap-ins.

Q: IS FITNESS AS IMPORTANT AS EVERYBODY MAKES OUT?
Alan: A striker must be able to jump above defenders, he must be able to accelerate, lose his marker and be alert. That comes from fitness training. You never stop learning no matter what level you are playing at and how long you've been playing.

Robbie Fowler

Q&A

Robbie Fowler emerged as one of England's finest goalscorers in a super season which catapulted him to international fame. SHOOT grabbed a word or two with the little Scouser who has set the season alight with a glut of glorious goals...

SHOOT: WERE YOU NURTURED BY LIVERPOOL AT AN EARLY AGE
Robbie: I was at the centre of excellence from when I was 11 to 14, but I played for Liverpool Schoolboys as well. You can still play for school teams and Sunday League teams. It's not as if they take you away to programme you.

YOU WERE AN EVERTONIAN AS A KID WEREN'T YOU, SO WHO DID YOU PRETEND TO BE IN THE PLAYGROUND?
Robbie: For me, it was Graeme Sharp and Trevor Steven and, on the world stage, Maradona. Now kids are shouting my name and it's hard to take in.

WHAT SORT OF MUSIC ARE YOU INTO?
Robbie: I like Oasis (right), but just because a load of us went to Marbella with Robbie Williams, it doesn't mean we're big Take That fans.

WHAT'S YOUR BIGGEST FEAR?
Robbie: For every footballer it must be injury. I broke my leg a couple of years ago and it really sets you back.

LIVERPOOL LEGEND BILL SHANKLY ONCE SAID THAT PLAYERS ARE BORN NOT MADE - DO YOU AGREE?
Robbie: You've got to be born with a gift yeah, but for me it was an obsession as well. That's all I ever wanted to do, play football. It was all that practising with an orange down the marina.

WHICH CURRENT STRIKERS DO YOU RATE?
Robbie: Les Ferdinand and Alan Shearer are quality strikers, as are George Weah and Patrick Kluivert.

WHAT ARE ROY EVANS AND THE REST OF THE STAFF LIKE?
Robbie: They all have these little red books in their pockets called 'Football Cliches'. If we're playing

rubbish they do lose their temper - and so they should. But half the time you can't hear them with the crowd.

WHAT ARE LIVERPOOL v MAN. UTD GAMES LIKE TO PLAY IN?
Robbie: They are great to play in and the rivalry's really good, which makes it even more exciting.

DIDN'T YOU COME CLOSE TO JOINING EVERTON ONCE?
Robbie: I was in a city centre hotel having a chat with a financial adviser and Joe Royle came in so I had a drink with him. The next thing the rumours were flying that I was going to sign for Everton.

WHAT'S YOUR VIEW OF GRAEME SOUNESS?
Robbie: I made my debut after Liverpool had just been beaten in a derby match. I respect Graeme Souness for bringing me into the side and giving me a chance. I think he wanted what was best for the club. He was a hard man and everyone knew that.

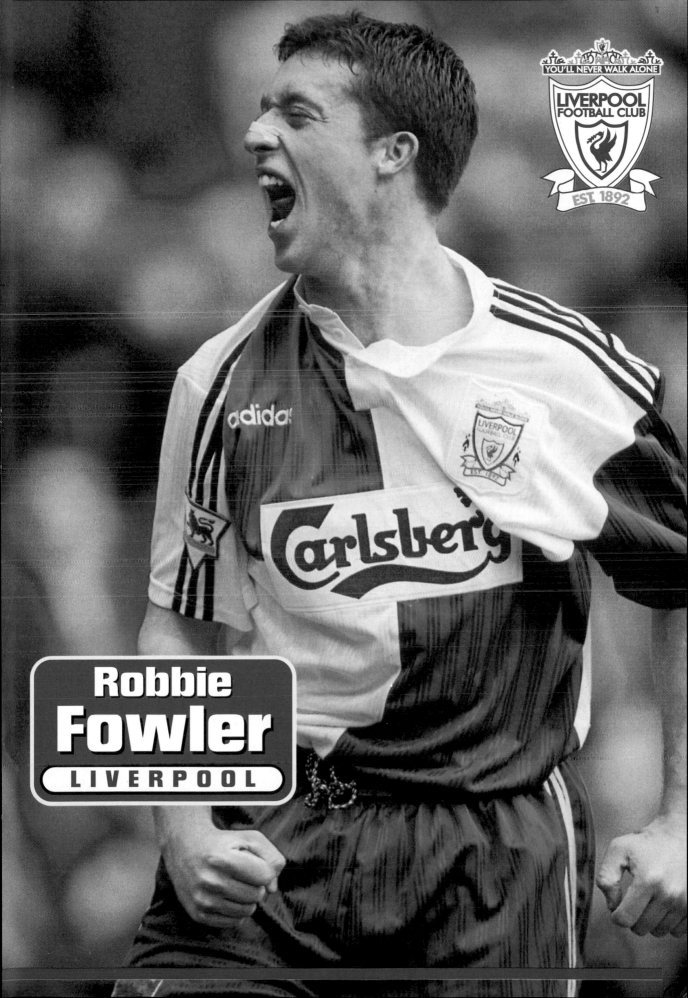

YOU'LL NEVER WALK ALONE

LIVERPOOL
FOOTBALL CLUB

EST 1892

Robbie Fowler

LIVERPOOL

Dwight Yorke

Q&A

Trinidad star Dwight Yorke had a marvellous season last year by any standards. His goal filled campaign was topped by a terrific strike in Villa's 3-0 Coca-Cola Cup thrashing of Leeds. Here's what dynamic Dwight says about his exploits in what was the best season of his career...

YOUR FORM LAST SEASON - WAS IT YOUR BEST EVER?
Dwight: Yes, I think so, particularly on a consistent basis. But then playing every week does help to show people what you are capable of. Prior to that I probably used to play a few games then get left out, or come in for when people were injured. It was all part of my learning experience.

WHAT WAS IT LIKE UNDER RON ATKINSON?
Dwight: You look at the whole thing and you look at the players he bought...Dean Saunders, Dalian Atkinson etc., and I had to compete against them. Luckily enough I was able to play in several positions and I will never blame Ron for anything.

HAVE YOU ALWAYS BEEN A STRIKER?
Dwight: I came to Villa as a striker but I would have done anything to be playing in the team week-in and week-out and if it actually meant me going in goal I would have done.

WHAT WAS THE SECRET OF YOUR SUCCESS LAST TERM?
Dwight: I've been very positive and the guys the gaffer brought in, together with the system he introduced, was excellent. Everybody is on the same wavelength.

HOW HARD WAS IT FOR SAVO MILOSEVIC?
Dwight: It takes anybody a length of time to settle in when they come from a foreign country, not just the food but the culture, the people, and the way of life is different and it takes a while to get used to all this. But he still proved how good he is and he will get even better.

WHAT ABOUT THAT PENALTY AGAINST SHEFFIELD UNITED IN THE FA CUP...COOL OR WHAT?
Dwight: I was confident I could do it. But I can tell you a little secret. When I put the ball down and I faced Alan Kelly I thought the distance looked longer between the spot and him than when I do it in training, the gap didn't feel as long but I thought 'I can still do it'. So I composed myself and luckily enough it went in. To try

something like that in the position we were in with the scores level was outrageous. After the game, Brian Little asked me to be a bit more ruthless and hit the ball as hard as possible and make sure it goes in next time.

WHAT DID WINNING THE COCA-COLA CUP MEAN TO YOU?
Dwight: A great deal because I was left out of the side when we beat Manchester United in 1994 and that hurt. I can still remember Ron Atkinson's exact words to me... they were 'I know you are disappointed and everything but just make sure when you come back here you are in the team'. Those words have always remained with me and always will and I was delighted to go back, play and win, and score a goal to cap it off.

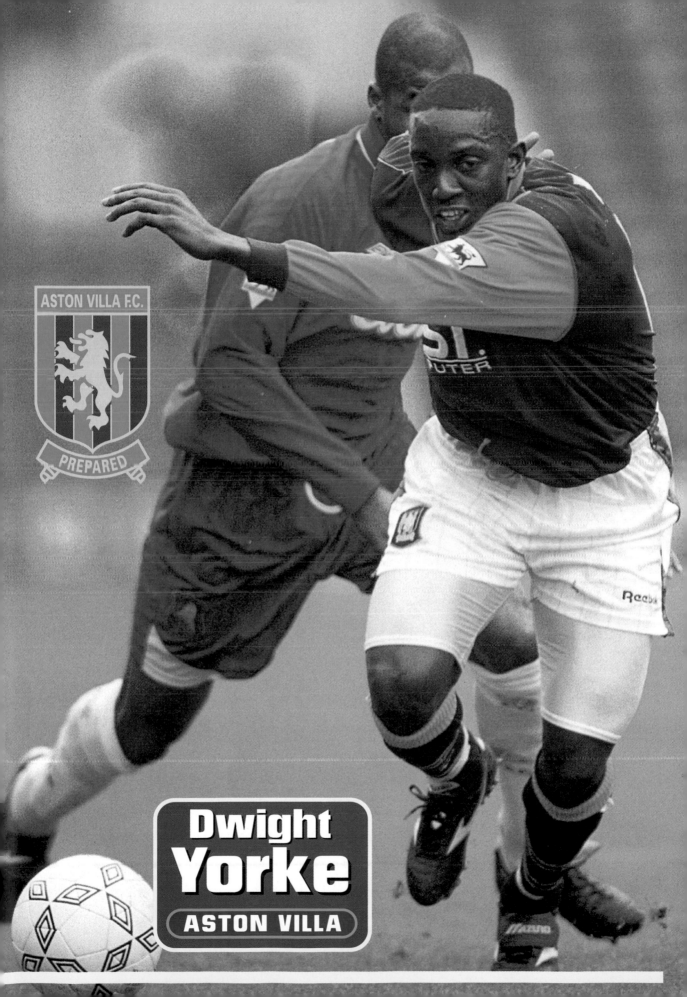

Dwight Yorke
ASTON VILLA

Pierre Van Hooydonk

Q&A

He's been a stunning success for Celtic since his arrival from NAC Breda and his goals have helped them launch a serious challenge to Rangers for the first time in years. SHOOT grabbed a word with the dynamic Dutchman to get his views on a number of things...

DO YOU GET ANNOYED WITH THE PRESS?
Pierre: Not at all. It's part and parcel of the game. When you are young, you want to be successful and when you are successful you have to handle these things. It's part of the business and you will miss it when you are not playing.

SCORING THE WINNER IN THE SCOTTISH CUP FINAL IN 1995 MUST HAVE A GREAT FEELING?
Pierre: After we'd won the Scottish Cup, I could see how

much this club means to the fans. There were as many crying as celebrating. Fans kept asking me for my autograph or picture as I sat by the pool on holiday and I got a standing ovation one time when I walked into a bar.

BUT DIDN'T YOU ONCE FEEL YOU HAD MADE A MISTAKE COMING TO THE CLUB?
Pierre: We didn't play good football and I remember one match with Aberdeen. We were 1-0 up and we made a couple of back passes. The crowd were shouting for us to get forward, but I think if you've got the ball, then the opposition can't score. That's something everyone in Holland finds easy to appreciate, but not here.

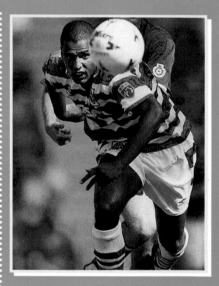

HOW DO YOU FEEL NOW?
Pierre: Now we are a good football side. If we are one-up, we knock the ball around and the fans shout 'Ole' at every pass. Tommy Burns must take a lot of credit for that. He had no fear about changing the style, yet there was always the risk we'd have ups and downs - and Celtic is a club where the fans find it hard to accept any downs.

YO' GAVE RANGERS A GOOD RUN FOR THEIR MONEY LAST SEASON DIDN'T YOU?
Pierre: We have closed the gap on them and if we keep on with this style, we'll be successful because skill always wins. I don't mean that Rangers are not skilful - they have good players, but a pure

passing team will win nine times out of ten against one which doesn't pass.

HOW DO YOU RATE ENGLISH FOOT-BALL?
Pierre: I see good strikers from England on TV. As a striker, I admire Aston Villa's Dwight Yorke and Newcastle's Les Ferdinand but, while the game can be exciting, they will never challenge the best in Europe.

WHAT DO YOU MEAN EXACTLY?
Pierre: Players abroad understand tactics better, even when they are young. One of the things you need to get rid of in Britain is school football. We don't have it in Holland, youngsters are taught by proper coaches.

THE CELTIC FOOTBALL CLUB 1888

Pierre
Van
Hooydonk
CELTIC

Teddy Sheringham

Q&A

Teddy Sheringham has become one of the most accomplished strikers in the Premiership and a regular England ace to boot. SHOOT grabbed ten minutes with the busy Spurs star to get his views on all manner of things...

HOW FAR AWAY ARE SPURS FROM BEING TITLE CONTENDERS:
Teddy: We've got a very good side, there is no doubt about that, and on our day we can match anyone. But to win the title you have got to have strength in depth and we haven't got that in the same way Man. Utd, Liverpool and Newcastle have.

WHAT'S CHRIS ARMSTRONG LIKE TO PLAY WITH?
Teddy: Chris is exceptionally quick and that's his main asset, and he's good in the air. He can also score goals and that's something you can't teach people. I would say he's still got a bit to learn, playing wise, but his raw talents are great and complement my style.

HOW GOOD DO YOU THINK THE PAIR OF YOU CAN GET?
Teddy: It's a different sort of partnership to the one I had with Jurgen Klinsmann. You can't take anything away from him because

he was a one-off, coming to England and doing what he did. This is a different partnership, you're starting again and life goes on. We've done quite well but hopefully things will get even better.

HOW MUCH FURTHER CAN SPURS GO NEXT SEASON?
Teddy: It will be another big season next year. You always think you could have done better and that there's progress to be made. But we are in this game to win things and we haven't done that yet. That's something we all want to put right as soon as possible.

WHICH 'KEEPER HAVE YOU FOUND IT HARD TO SCORE AGAINST?
Teddy: All of them. They are all extremely difficult to beat. If your team is not playing all that well and you're not getting the chances where you want them, then all of them are hard to score against.

APART FROM WHITE HART LANE, WHAT IS YOUR FAVOURITE STADIUM?
Teddy: It has to be Wembley, because it's so unique. And if you are playing there, you are either playing in a Cup Final or for England, so that makes it even more special.

WHO WAS YOUR IDOL WHEN YOU WERE YOUNG?
Teddy: I had two - Kenny Dalglish and Glenn Hoddle. Kenny because of his ability as a striker, and Glenn because he was just pure class.

HAVE YOU ALWAYS BEEN A STRIKER?
Teddy: No, I always used to play in midfield when I was a youngster but that was only so I could get more involved really. Once I started playing in better teams, I always played in attack to score the goals. That's the part of the game that everyone enjoys the most.

Teddy
Sheringham
TOTTENHAM

Ryan Giggs

Q&A

Ryan Giggs has proved he's still the best winger in the business after another fabulous season with Man United. Giggsy's skill and trickery had Premiership defences at sixes and sevens throughout United's successful campaign. SHOOT grabbed a word with the flying winger to check out all the latest news...

DO YOU WANT TO STAY AT UNITED?
Giggsy: I don't really have any ambitions to move. If you look at the Premiership now, there are such good players I don't think there is any need to go abroad.

HAVE YOU ALWAYS BEEN A UNITED SUPPORTER?
Giggsy: Yes, I've supported them since I was very young and have

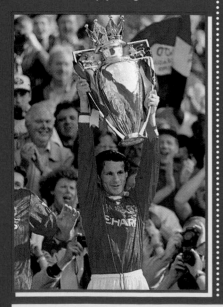

been lucky enough to play for them. I don't think there is really any bigger club in the world and I would love to stay here.

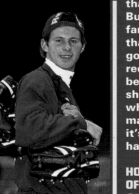

WHAT ARE YOUR VIEWS ON THE PREMIERSHIP?
Giggsy: In my opinion it is the best League in the world, especially now that Ruud Gullit, Dennis Bergkamp and Juninho, some of the best players in the world, are over here.

DO THE YOUNG LADS ASK YOU FOR ADVICE?
Giggsy: They don't ask for advice from me concerning things on the field, it's more like commercial deals and the other pressures. But they are intelligent enough to work it out for themselves.

HOW DO YOU COPE WITH THE PRESSURES ON THE PITCH?
Giggsy: Out on the field is the place where I feel the most comfortable. Every day I look forward to training hard and playing. There is pressure playing in front of so many people but it is where I can express myself, so I don't really feel it. Ever since I came into the team we have been challenging for the League or Cup.

AND OFF IT?
Giggsy: If I could change anything about being Ryan Giggs it would that. I don't mind if people are critical of the way I am playing,

that's their opinion. But when it's my family or private life that's different. It's got a lot worse recently. I used to be able to go shopping or whatever without many problems but it's something you have to get used to.

HOW DO YOU SWITCH OFF?
Giggsy: I enjoy being at home were I can just relax, or go to my friends' house or the local pub. Then there is no pressure at all.

WOULD YOU SWAP YOUR LIFESTYLE THOUGH FOR SOMETHING ELSE?
Giggsy: Sometimes I think I would like a quiet life, but I wouldn't change being a footballer.

WHAT ABOUT ERIC CANTONA?
Giggsy: He gives the team an extra dimension. When he plays we rarely lose and that has a great effect on us all. Having such a world class player in your team is bound to benefit your own game.

Ryan Giggs
Man Utd

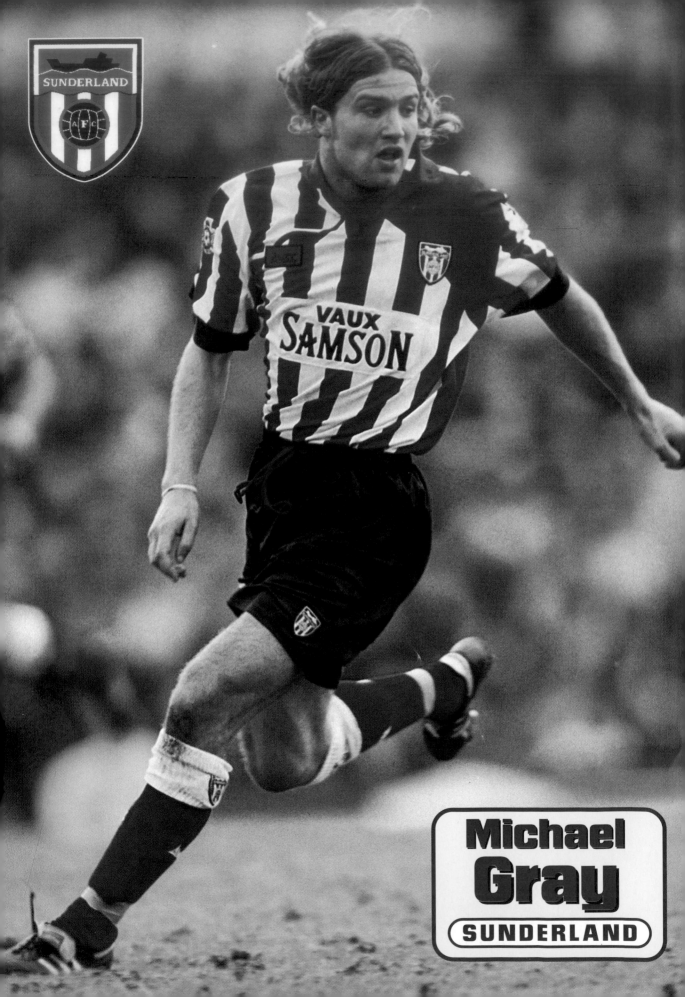

SUNDERLAND

VAUX SAMSON

Michael Gray

SUNDERLAND

REACHING FOR THE TOP

Welcome to our six page Endsleigh Extra

THEY SAY the gap between the Premiership and the Endsleigh League is growing all the time, but that did nothing to stop the thrills and spills out of the top flight.

Sunderland, Swindon and Preston took the three divisional titles, but the fight for two of the last automatic promotion places went right to the last kick of the season.

Derby overcame Crystal Palace's late challenge but, in the Second Division, Oxford stole Blackpool's First Division ticket right at the death.

In the Third, Gillingham had to settle for runners-up, while Darlington and Bury scrapped over the final promotion spot, with The Shakers clinching it on the final day.

The First Division was the tightest ever. Millwall led the table on December 9 1995, but by the final whistle at Ipswich on May 5, they were down to Division Two!

Watford were dead and buried with a month left, but Graham Taylor stirred them and they could have caught Portsmouth on the last day. At least they'll still have a derby match - Luton are back in the Second Division for the first time since 1970.

Torquay are still with us thanks to Stevenage's title triumph in the Conference, and Liverpool legend Jan Molby couldn't stop Swansea from joining them in Division Three.

But there's plenty of life outside the top flight - and we've brought it to you here.....

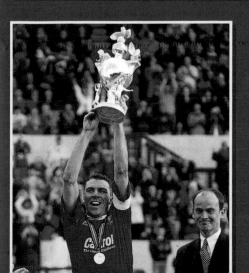

The HIT Men

Check out the Endsleigh's lethal marksmen

There are some things you can learn to do, but sticking the ball in the net isn't one of them. You've either got it or you haven't. And these six scoring sensations have certainly got it - and more. Defenders dread coming up against this lot - find out why.....

DOUGIE FREEDMAN

CRYSTAL PALACE

1995-96: 23 League goals for Crystal Palace
Freed by QPR in 1994, Dougie had a storming first season in the League for Barnet, scoring 24 times. That led Crystal Palace to pay £800,000 for the Scottish Under-21 international in September 1995. After a slow start, Freedman reacted to Dave Bassett's appointment as manager with an acceleration in the goals stakes.

He matched last season's total as Palace stormed up the table and into the Play-Offs, as Bassett gave him the responsibility of being Palace's main striker, rather than sharing the task with Gareth Taylor and Bruce Dyer.

JOHN ALDRIDGE

TRANMERE

1995-96: 27 League goals for Tranmere
What can you say about a man who makes scoring goals look as easy as picking fruit? The ball goes into the box and Aldo knocks it into the net. Simple as that. And he's done it more than 330 times in League football with Newport, Oxford, Liverpool, Real Sociedad and Tranmere. At nearly 38, Aldridge has defied the years. Only Ray Wilkins can beat Aldo as the oldest player-manager in the League, but even Butch gave up international football long ago - John was still playing for the Republic of Ireland at 37!

His amazing 27 goals in 1995-96 kept Tranmere in Division One and he was rewarded with the player-manager's role late in the season, with long-term boss John King moving upstairs at Prenton Park. Respect is due.

DEAN STURRIDGE

DERBY

1995-96: 20 League goals for Derby
The way Dean Sturridge started last season, you'd have thought he had something to prove. Well, he had. The Brummie striker hardly got a look-in at the Baseball Ground the season before, but new boss Jim Smith gave Sturridge a chance - and, boy, did he take it!

Five goals in the opening seven games were about the only highlight as Derby made a poor start, but his goals disappeared until the turning point in November - a 3-0 win over West Brom that started a run of 20 games without defeat, with Sturridge scoring ten times in that run as The Rams headed for the Premiership

A third-minute opener put them on their way in the promotion clincher against Palace and Dean had made his point good and proper!

ANDY SAVILLE

PRESTON

1995-96: 29 League goals for Preston
Seventy-five goals in ten years is hardly prolific stuff for a striker. But Andy Saville's all-round game made him a favourite at Hull, Barnsley and Hartlepool before Barry Fry took him to Birmingham City.

Preston laid out £75,000 for Saville's services in 1995, and were delighted to cough up another £25,000 when he notched his 15th goal before Christmas! Savo grabbed two hat-tricks as North End became the League's top scorers and surged towards the Second Division.

While the second half of the campaign saw PNE struggle to repeat early form, there was no stopping Saville. He scored the goals that won them promotion and the title, and ended with 30 in total for the season. Not bad for a 32-year-old, slow, baldie!

STEVE WHITE

HEREFORD

1995-96: 29 League goals for Hereford
The Peter Pan of English football, Steve White looks exactly the same as he did when he first started scoring for Bristol Rovers nearly 20 years ago!

Thirty-eight-years-old at New Year, White has scored nearly all of his goals in the south-west and, last s eason, his astonishing late burst took Hereford from the bottom half of the table into the Play-Off zone.

Nine goals in six Spring games took White over the 200 mark for League goals, and with four in 90 minutes against Cambridge and a hat-trick in the promotion cruncher with Plymouth to look back on, 1995-96 was a great season for one of the Endsleigh League's greatest goalscorers.

GARY MARTINDALE

NOTTS COUNTY

1995-96: 21 League goals for Notts County and Peterborough
Gary who? You may well ask. At the start of last season, the Liverpool lad was given a free by Bolton. He got a job with Peterborough in Division Two and made his League debut aged 24 - and scored!

The Posh were struggling in front of goal but at least Martindale was finding the target. After an amazing 18 goals in his first seven months of first team football, Martindale was heading to promotion-chasers Notts County in a £175,000 deal.

He scored six more League goals for County as they reached the Play-Offs and now, after a late start to his career, he will be hoping to make up for lost time.

Cheer up Peter Reid

Sunderland storm into Premiership

WHEN SUNDERLAND won promotion to the Premiership without even playing, it was a complete shock to Peter Reid. The Roker leader was watching Darlington v Bury and was so engrossed in the game that he didn't take any notice of Derby's draw with Birmingham. When told Sunderland were up, the former Everton star said: "I didn't even realise we could go up today!"

The party started on Wearside, to bring a glorious end to an amazing year at Roker Park. In March 1995, Reid was brought in to keep Sunderland in Division One. He did it, and without the multi-million pounds spent by neighbour Kevin Keegan when he did the same for Newcastle.

And his achievements last season were even greater, as Sunderland made complete a trio of north-eastern clubs in the top flight for the first time for 20 years. On that occasion, Sunderland went straight back down, as they did in 1991. Reid must prove wrong everyone who thinks there will be a repeat performance this time around.

A year ago, the whole future of the club was in doubt. Next year, they move into a new 34,000-seater stadium. Now that's Mackam magic.

THE CRUNCHERS

THE GAMES THAT WON IT FOR SUNDERLAND;

DECEMBER 6, 1995 SUNDERLAND 6 MILLWALL 0
Leaders Millwall were humbled at Roker by four-goal Craig Russell.

FEBRUARY 17, 1996 PORTSMOUTH 2 SUNDERLAND 2
Lee Howey's last-minute equaliser won a rare point after the FA Cup defeat by Man United. Sunderland won their next nine games!

MARCH 9, 1996 SUNDERLAND 3 DERBY 0
That man Russell got two again as nearest challengers Derby were seen off in style.

APRIL 6, 1996 BARNSLEY 0 SUNDERLAND 1
Russell scored, of course, and theChampionship race was all but over - and the champagne was on ice.

APRIL 21, 1996 SUNDERLAND 0 STOKE 0
Yet another goalless draw at Roker, but no-one cared? Reid's army were up, and the party was on!

THE KEY MAN
MICHAEL BRIDGES

TEENAGE SENSATION Bridges is being talked about as Roker's own Robbie Fowler. A speedy striker, Bridges' super-sub appearances took Sunderland by storm in 1996. Called up for England Under-18s at only 16, Peter Reid ripped up Michael's YTS forms and captured him on a pro contract after an amazing scoring run in the juniors. Reid handed him a first team debut at 17, and boyhood hero Alan Shearer rang to congratulate him!

In his first eight games as sub, Michael scored four times as Sunderland stormed to the Premiership. Now he looks set to form a fiercesome attacking trio with Phil Gray and Craig Russell.

Jim's Grand Ram Slam

THEY'D SEEN IT all before at Derby. A manager comes in and spends a fortune but the team of moneybags go nowhere. This time, Jim Smith spent £5m - but he financed it all by selling players and, by November, it all gelled together. Dean Sturridge started scoring up front, Robin Van Der Laan settled into midfield and, most importantly, Croatian skipper Igor Stimac, bought from Hajduk Split for £1.5m, shored up the defence.

From then on in, Derby were on a roll. Sturridge, Marco Gabbiadini and Ron Willems shared out the goals, but it was the defence, with the exception of a 3-0 thrashing at Sunderland, that put them in contention for an automatic slot.

They did it with a game to spare when Palace came to the Baseball Ground needing to win to gazump The Rams. But County just snatched it thanks to Dutch star Van Der Laan.

Now, like Sunderland, their aim is to stay in the Premiership and move into their new stadium.

"I've read that we need to spend £20m on players to stay in the Premiership," says chairman Lionel Pickering. "I haven't got £20m, but Jim Smith will pull a few continentals out of the hat."

THE KEY MAN
IGOR STIMAC

AFTER SCORING in the thrashing at Tranmere, Igor Stimac turned his attentions to sorting out a Derby defence that was threatening to ruin their season. In the next 16 games, County conceded only ten goals, and Stimac was the man to thank for that. His experience and strength was a massive influence and gave The Rams the confidence to go forward in numbers. Captain of his country at Euro 96, Stimac is a class buy at a bargain price and will grace the top flight.

Return of the

Steve's Swindon bounce back up

W **STEVE MCMAHON** knows what it's like to win things. Like Peter Reid at Sunderland, McMahon knew little about the lower leagues when he took over as player-manager at the County Ground. Unlike Reid, he couldn't stop them from sliding into Division Two. But they bounced back in style, playing attractive football with a killer instinct - few clubs scored more goals than them, and no-one in Division Two had a tighter defence.

At first the goals came from Steve Finney, then Wayne Allison took over. Peter Thorne hit the goal path to drag them out of a New Year hangover and Kevin Horlock ended the season in stunning fashion, with goals galore.

They rarely looked like slipping up and clinched promotion at Blackpool with four games to go. The title was sealed at Chesterfield and the party began.

But Robins' fans could do with a quiet season in Division One - this up and down business is no good for your heart!

THE KEY MAN
KEVIN HORLOCK

South Londoner Kevin learnt the game at West Ham, but didn't get a first team chance before heading to Swindon in 1992-93. He didn't play in their Wembley Play-Off win in his first season, but followed that promotion with a full season in the Premiership. Relegation followed relegation but Kevin was rewarded with his first Northern Ireland cap. A former defender, he was converted into a wide man who gets forward. Last season, his 16 goals showed how dangerous he is, and his loyalty over four yo-yo years have made him a key member of the side.

THE CRUNCHERS

THE GAMES THAT WON IT FOR SWINDON:

September 13
SWINDON 4 BRADFORD 1
A demolition of a highly-regarded Bradford side showed why Town were top, with the goals all shared out. They repeated the scoreline at Bristol Rovers three days later.

October 21 SWINDON 2 CREWE 1
A very late penalty from Steve Finney clinched all three points in this promotion clash.

January 20 SWINDON 3 HULL 0
Not an amazing result - but it brought to an end a sticky run of only two wins in ten weeks. It was plain-sailing from then on.

February 28 SOUTHAMPTON 2 SWINDON 0
This FA Cup Fifth Round replay defeat made Town concentrate on the League, but they'd proved their class and given the Saints a tough tie.

March 23 SWINDON 2 PETERBOROUGH 0
This quiet win came straight after a 3-0 thrashing at Oxford, when the critics started to question Swindon's credentials.

April 20 BLACKPOOL 1 SWINDON 1
A bad-tempered reaction by Blackpool almost spoiled the Robins' party. This draw clinched it, thanks to yet another Kevin Horlock strike.

Mac

A tale of two cities and a season of two halves. Oxford were superb at home, but until the New Year, couldn't do the business away from the Manor Ground.

At New Year, they were in the bottom half of Division Two. But the arrival of Martin Aldridge from Northampton eased their scoring problems and they started to scrape points together, while taking Nottingham Forest to a Fourth Round replay in the FA Cup.

From February onward, there was no stopping Dennis Smith's team. Paul Moody got back on the goal trail and David Rush joined in the fun with a string of goals.

One defeat in the last 17 games, and four defeats in 24 League games in 1996, took United from mid-table into the Play-Off places.

And an Easter win over Blackpool put them within reach of the top two - Blackpool started to shake and Oxford pounced, winning the last game of the season to clinch promotion.

"I knew I had a good side," said Smith. "This proves I was right to stick by my principles. People wanted me out at Christmas but the lads were magnificent and deserved everything they got."

The late late show

Oxford snatch ticket to top

THE CRUNCHERS

November 4 OXFORD 2 BRISTOL CITY 0
United were nowhere in Division Two but two late goals ended a four-match run without a win.

February 24 CARLISLE 1 OXFORD 2
A last minute winner from Martin Aldridge took the points. It was only their second away win. Then the run of form begins...

March 19 OXFORD 3 SWINDON 0
A thrilling win over the Champions-elect kept Oxford well placed into the Play-Offs.

April 6 OXFORD 1 BLACKPOOL 0
Joey Beauchamp's late winner put Oxford within reach of the top two. Blackpool crashed again two days later and were leapfrogged.

May 4 OXFORD 1 PETERBOROUGH 0
A win saw Oxford pip Blackpool to the second promotion spot. It took an age for the breakthrough but then the goals flowed and United were up!

THE KEY MAN
MARTIN ALDRIDGE

After two promising seasons with Northampton, 22-year-old Aldridge was struggling last season and was loaned out to Conference side Dagenham & Redbridge. Dennis Smith rescued him from there at New Year and nine goals in the run-in showed his ability in midfield or up front.

This season, Aldridge will be playing Division One football - while former team-mates Dagenham are down in the Icis League. What a strange world.

Up, up and away

Preston reign on the road

Preston had had to wait 25 years to win something - and they weren't going to let it pass unnoticed.

Nearly 19,000 fans packed the new Deepdale to watch the Third Division Championship trophy paraded, but it was on the road that Preston won the title.

After clinching promotion at Orient - an exact repeat of their 1987 feat - manager Gary Peters went to his sister's 40th birthday party while the rest of Preston partied. When they won the Championship a week later at Hartlepool, he said: "This club has been starved of success for a long time and if I can be remembered for helping win this title, I'll die happy."

Peters had built a team virtually unbeatable away from the pressure of big, expectant crowds at Deepdale, and after losing at home on the opening day, they went 21 League games unbeaten.

Too many draws left them still uncertain of an automatic promotion place and when the goals packed-up, they staggered over the final furlongs. Three more home defeats contrasted with a fantastic away record - the best in the club's 115-year history.

Andy Saville's goals saw them cross the line eventually, just ahead of Gillingham.

"A successful team is one that does it again the next season," claimed Peters. Preston fans are looking to do just that.

THE KEY MAN
Simon Davey

WELSH MIDFIELDER Davey has had a whirlwind two years. Given a free by Swansea, he was captain of Carlisle when he left their all-conquering side in 1995 to join Preston. A shaky start to 1995-96 left North End fans wondering if Davey was all he first seemed to be. But as Preston's promotion push gathered pace, Davey's performances got better and better.

He cleaned up in midfield, passed the ball superbly and made runs into the box which David Platt would be proud of. He provided many of Andy Saville's goals and hit double figures himself, and for the second successive year, won the title and selection for the PFA Third Division team.

Gills Thrills

Gillingham lead the Third Division nearly all season and only Preston could snatch the title off them. And they did.

A year earlier, Gillingham were 24 hours from going under. But a takeover was followed by manager Tony Pulis building a new side, based on a rock solid defence. So solid that 'keeper Jim Stannard kept 28 clean sheets in the League campaign!

Record-breaking Jim picked the ball out of the net at Priestfield only six times all season, but the lack of goals scored by front-runners Dennis Bailey, Leo Fortune-West and Steve Butler cost them dear.

Once Big Jim finally let a couple past him, the Gills let the title slip away.

Promotion was gained however and they were joined in Division Two by Bury, who beat Cardiff 3-0 in the final game and had to wait to hear whether Darlington had won at Scunthorpe. They hadn't and The Shakers had won the race in a photo finish.

Quizimodo

Test your soccer knowledge to the full with our quiz section that is guaranteed to give you the 'ump!

QUIZZES CROSSWORDS COMPETITIONS PUZZLES

Quick off the mark

We start with 10 quick fire questions. You have one minute to answer the lot.

1. Who won the First Division in 1995-96?

2. For which Italian club did Gazza play?

3. Stan Collymore (left) created what record in the summer of 1995?

4. Which Scottish club are nicknamed The Jam Tarts?

5. For which country is Alessandro Del Piero an international?

6. At which ground do Nottingham Forest (right) play their home games?

7. Ruud Gullit left which club to join Chelsea?

8. Manchester City's chairman is Francis or Freddie Lee?

9. Who replaced Ron Atkinson (left) as manager at Aston Villa?

10. Which club finished runners-up in the 1995 Coca-Cola Cup Final?

All Quizimodo answers on page 125

The competition page that could give you the 'ump!

Quizimodo

WORDSEARCH

A	R	S	E	N	A	L	W	T	B
S	L	E	E	D	S	M	A	N	T
T	W	E	S	T	H	A	M	M	L
O	L	I	V	E	R	P	O	O	L
N	E	W	C	A	S	T	L	E	C
V	O	T	T	M	B	S	V	V	H
I	M	A	N	U	T	D	U	E	E
L	R	R	Y	M	O	K	W	R	L
L	D	E	R	B	Y	O	M	T	S
A	D	E	E	B	O	B	N	O	E
B	L	A	C	K	B	U	R	N	A

Hidden in the grid are the names of ten Premiership clubs. You can read them vertically, horizontally or diagonally. Can you spot them?

On The Ball

Tackle the questions (right) and fill in the initial letters to each answer on the ball provided on the numbers shown. The first one has been done for you. When the puzzle is completed, another star name can be found in the ball, running clockwise but not necessarily starting at No.1.

Coca-Cola Cup Winners 1992/93 The Coca-Cola

Missing Link

Fill in the missing gap with a name to create the identity of two stars.

Steve ———— Dyer
David ———— Quinn
Robert ———— Sharpe
Craig ———— Beardsmore
Tony ———— Bergkamp
Charlie ———— Barmby
Marvin ———— Robson
Bryan ———— Keane
Derek ———— Johnston
Jason ———— Dixon

Questions

On The Ball

1. *Who scored Bolton's goal in their 1995 Coca-Cola Cup defeat by Liverpool (6,8).*

2. *Ron Atkinson described this Villa star as one of the strongest players in British football. Who is he? (5,2)*

3. *Who skippered Arsenal to FA Cup and Coca-Cola Cup victory in 1993? (4,11)*

4. *Whose goal gave the FA Cup to Manchester United last season (10,1)*

5. *And who got the goal to give Everton the Cup the previous year? (9,12)*

6. *Did Stuart Ripley, Alan Shearer or Tim Sherwood leave Middlesbrough to join Blackburn? (3,7)*

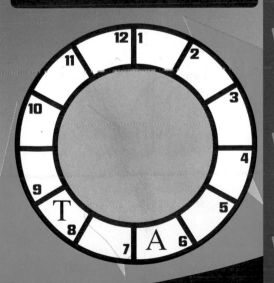

'ave a WORD Xword

diadora

ACROSS
1. A Rangers great who has made over 50 international appearances for Scotland (4,7)
7. Nick of Oldham (5)
8. The 1995 Coca-Cola Cup runners-up (5)
9. They were in Scotland's Euro 96 group (7)
12. - Rotterdam or - Prague (6)
15. It's not art from Doug of Motherwell (anag) (6)
16. Barcelona and Spanish star defender (5)
17. Juve ace who could be one of the stars of Euro 96 (3,5)
20. Ian -, made his name as a goalscorer with Tranmere (4)
21. Mark - Leeds' 'keeper who was sent-off at Old Trafford last term. (6)

DOWN
1. He joined Derby from Norwich in a £1 million deal (6,4)
2. Andy at Arsenal or David at Blackpool (8)
3. It's Cup Final month for a Manchester United player! (3)
4. Gary -, who makes it kid's stuff at Grimsby (6)
5. Former Manchester United and West Ham star (4)
6. This decides who has kick-off (4)
10. Nationality of Sturm Graz (8)
11. Arsenal midfield star (7)
13. A bottle of milk with nothing to follow for a Portuguese star? (5)
14. He scored Everton's winner in the 1995 FA Cup Final (7)
18. Rob -, Charlton star who left for Newcastle (3)
19. Dutchman at Nottingham Forest (3)
ANSWERS ON PAGE 125

Quizimodo Identity Parade

Use the clues to help you identify the mystery stars

1. There is Norway you shouldn't spot this Boro striker!

2. This great Dane is rated as the best in his position in Europe

3. Spurred Tottenham on in 1994-95 but then returned home

4. He was accused of losing his head last season

5. Former Cambridge defender who became a Don

6. Pacey star at Elland Road who has been capped by Wales

7. This Toffees striker was gutted at missing Euro 96

8. Tottenham swooped for this Eagle in the summer of 1995

9. Was accused of having a pineapple on his head at Forest

10. Shear class took his club Rover the moon in 1995

Quizimodo

A Question of sport

Picture Board
Study the pictures and tell us who the mystery stars are.

A

B

C

Mystery Guest
Can you spot the golfer who teed off with a glut of goals last term?

What happened next?
We've frozen the action during one of the big matches of 1996. What followed?

Home or Away
Tackle the home question on British football or the away one on a continental star.

Home: Who scored the opening goal in last season's Coca-Cola Cup Final?

Away: Alessandro Del Piero is an international for Italy, Spain or France?

One minute round......

You have 60 seconds to answer the following questions.

1. At which ground do Nottingham Forest play their home games?
2. Which club did Ruud Gullit leave to join Chelsea?
3. Who scored Arsenal's FA Cup winner against Sheffield Wednesday in 1993?
4. Name the Scottish club nicknamed The Jam Tarts.
5. The following three internationals all bring a touch of colour to the game.
Can you fill in the surnames?

a) David ————— England

b) Kingsley ————— N.Ireland

c) Jamie ————— England

Paul Gascoigne

RANGERS

SCOTTISH FOOTBALLER OF THE YEAR 1996

TAKE STAT

All the facts and figures on your club as they finished the 1996 season

PREMIERSHIP

ARSENAL

Top League scorer:	Ian Wright (15)
League goals scored:	49
League goals conceded:	32
Highest attendance:	38,323 v Liverpool
Lowest attendance:	34,519 v Man City
Average attendance:	37,568
Total sendings-off:	2
Total bookings:	63

ASTON VILLA

Top League scorer:	Dwight Yorke (17)
League goals scored:	52
League goals conceded:	35
Highest attendance:	39,336 v Man City
Lowest attendance:	23,933 v Middlesbro'
Average attendance:	32,771
Total sendings-off:	2
Total bookings:	41

Dwight Yorke

BLACKBURN

Top League scorer:	Alan Shearer (31)
League goals scored:	61
League goals conceded:	47
Highest attendance:	30,895 v Liverpool
Lowest attendance:	22,860 v QPR
Average attendance:	27,552
Total sendings-off:	5
Total bookings:	65

BOLTON

Top League scorer:	John McGinlay (6)
League goals scored:	39
League goals conceded:	71
Highest attendance:	21,381 v Man Utd
Lowest attendance:	16,216 v Wimbledon
Average attendance:	18,822
Total sendings-off:	3
Total bookings:	60

John Spencer

CHELSEA

Top League scorer:	John Spencer (13)
League goals scored:	46
League goals conceded:	44
Highest attendance:	31,137 v Liverpool
Lowest attendance:	17,078 v Man City
Average attendance:	25,597
Total sendings-off:	3
Total bookings:	65

COVENTRY

Top League scorer:	Dion Dublin (14)
League goals scored:	42
League goals conceded:	60
Highest attendance:	23,400 v Man Utd
Lowest attendance:	12,523 v Wimbledon
Average attendance:	18,527
Total sendings-off:	3
Total bookings:	60

Eight page fact filled review of 95-96

EVERTON

Top League scorer:	A. Kanchelskis (16)
League goals scored:	64
League goals conceded:	44
Highest attendance:	40,127 v Aston Villa
Lowest attendance:	30,009 v QPR
Average attendance:	35,424
Total sendings-off:	3
Total bookings:	65

LEEDS

Top League scorer:	Tony Yeboah (12)
League goals scored:	40
League goals conceded:	57
Highest attendance:	39,801 v Man Utd
Lowest attendance:	26,077 v Soton
Average attendance:	32,628
Total sendings-off:	4
Total bookings:	61

Tony Yeboah

LIVERPOOL

Top League scorer: Robbie Fowler (28)	
League goals scored:	70
League goals conceded:	34
Highest attendance: 40,820 v Chelsea	
Lowest attendance: 34,063 v Wimbledon	
Average attendance:	39,552
Total sendings-off:	0
Total bookings:	40

MAN CITY

Top League scorer: Uwe Rosler (9)	
League goals scored:	33
League goals conceded:	58
Highest attendance: 31,436 v Liverpool	
Lowest attendance: 23,617 v Wimbledon	
Average attendance:	27,941
Total sendings-off:	6
Total bookings:	67

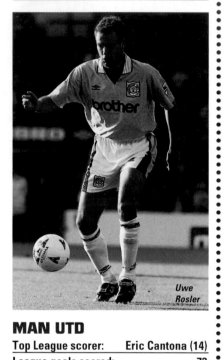

Uwe Rosler

MAN UTD

Top League scorer: Eric Cantona (14)	
League goals scored:	73
League goals conceded:	35
Highest attendance: 53,926 v Nottm For	
Lowest attendance: 31,966 v West Ham	
Average attendance:	41,681
Total sendings-off:	3
Total bookings:	50

MIDDLESBROUGH

Top League scorer: Nick Barmby (7)	
League goals scored:	35
League goals conceded:	50
Highest attendance: 30,011 v Newcastle	
Lowest attendance: 27,882 v Coventry	
Average attendance:	29,256
Total sendings-off:	3
Total bookings:	73

NEWCASTLE

Top League scorer: Les Ferdinand (25)	
League goals scored:	66
League goals conceded:	37
Highest attendance: 36,589 v Tottenham	
Lowest attendance: 36,225 v Chelsea	
Average attendance:	36,505
Total sendings-off:	1
Total bookings:	47

Les Ferdinand

NOTTM FOR

Top League scorer: Ian Woan, Jason Lee, Bryan Roy (8)	
League goals scored:	50
League goals conceded:	54
Highest attendance: 29,263 v Man Utd	
Lowest attendance: 20,810 v Wimbledon	
Average attendance:	25,915
Total sendings-off:	2
Total bookings:	45

QPR

Top League scorer: Daniele Dichio (10)	
League goals scored:	38
League goals conceded:	57
Highest attendance: 18,828 v West Ham	
Lowest attendance: 11,189 v Coventry	
Average attendance:	15,672
Total sendings-off:	4
Total bookings:	72

SHEFF WED

Top League scorer: David Hirst (13)	
League goals scored:	48
League goals conceded:	61
Highest attendance: 34,101 v Man Utd	
Lowest attendance: 16,229 v Coventry	
Average attendance:	24,873
Total sendings-off:	1
Total bookings:	36

SOUTHAMPTON

Top League scorer: Neil Shipperley, Matt Le Tissier (7)	
League goals scored:	34
League goals conceded:	52
Highest attendance: 15,262 v Man Utd	
Lowest attendance: 13,216 v Sheff Wed	
Average attendance:	14,821
Total sendings-off:	2
Total bookings:	59

TOTTENHAM

Top League scorer: Teddy Shering'm (16)	
League goals scored:	50
League goals conceded:	38
Highest attendance: 32,918 v Chelsea	
Lowest attendance: 25,321 v Wimbledon	
Average attendance:	30,548
Total sendings-off:	0
Total bookings:	53

WEST HAM

Top League scorer: Julian Dicks, Tony Cottee (10)	
League goals scored:	43
League goals conceded:	52
Highest attendance: 24,324 v Liverpool	
Lowest attendance: 18,501 v So'ton	
Average attendance:	22,316
Total sendings-off:	4
Total bookings:	52

Tony Cottee

WIMBLEDON

Top League scorer: Robbie Earle (11)	
League goals scored:	55
League goals conceded:	70
Highest attendance: 25,380 v Man Utd	

Lowest attendance:	6,352 v Sheff Wed
Average attendance:	13,232
Total sendings-off:	8
Total bookings:	53

ENDSLEIGH FIRST DIVISION

BARNSLEY

Top League scorer:	Andy Payton (17)
League goals scored:	60
League goals conceded:	66
Highest attendance:	13,669 v Leicester
Lowest attendance:	5,488 v Reading
Average attendance:	8,118
Total sendings-off:	3
Total bookings:	51

Jonathan Hunt

BIRMINGHAM

Top League scorer:	Jonathan Hunt (11)
League goals scored:	61
League goals conceded:	64
Highest attendance:	23,251 v Sunderland
Lowest attendance:	14,368 v Barnsley
Average attendance:	18,106
Total sendings-off:	0
Total bookings:	45

C.PALACE

Top League scorer:	Doug Freedman (20)
League goals scored:	67
League goals conceded:	48
Highest attendance:	19,354 v Norwich
Lowest attendance:	11,548 v Grimsby
Average attendance:	14,600
Total sendings-off:	4
Total bookings:	67

Carl Leaburn

CHARLTON

Top League scorer:	Carl Leaburn (9)
League goals scored:	57
League goals conceded:	45
Highest attendance:	14,653 v Luton
Lowest attendance:	7,804 v Reading
Average attendance:	11,200
Total sendings-off:	4
Total bookings:	67

DERBY

Top League scorer:	Dean Sturridge (20)
League goals scored:	71
League goals conceded:	51
Highest attendance:	17,460 v Wolves
Lowest attendance:	9,242 v Southend
Average attendance:	14,327
Total sendings-off:	0
Total bookings:	62

GRIMSBY

Top League scorer:	S. Livingstone (11)
League goals scored:	55
League goals conceded:	69
Highest attendance:	8,155 v West Brom
Lowest attendance:	3,993 v Watford
Average attendance:	5,865
Total sendings-off:	2
Total bookings:	42

HUDDERSFIELD

Top League scorer:	Andy Booth (16)
League goals scored:	61
League goals conceded:	58
Highest attendance:	18,495 v Derby
Lowest attendance:	10,556 v Watford
Average attendance:	13,150
Total sendings-off:	6
Total bookings:	54

IPSWICH

Top League scorer:	Ian Marshall (19)
League goals scored:	79
League goals conceded:	69
Highest attendance:	20,355 v Norwich
Lowest attendance:	9,123 v Luton
Average attendance:	12,587
Total sendings-off:	4
Total bookings:	49

LEICESTER

Top League scorer:	Iwan Roberts (19)
League goals scored:	66
League goals conceded:	60
Highest attendance:	20,911 v Derby
Lowest attendance:	12,543 v Millwall
Average attendance:	16,197
Total sendings-off:	2
Total bookings:	58

LUTON

Top League scorer:	Bontcho Guentchev, Dwight Marshall (9)
League goals scored:	40
League goals conceded:	64
Highest attendance:	9,454 v Watford
Lowest attendance:	5,443 v Port Vale
Average attendance:	7,223
Total sendings-off:	4
Total bookings:	77

MILLWALL

Top League scorer:	Alex Rae (13)
League goals scored:	43
League goals conceded:	63
Highest attendance:	14,220 v Port Vale
Lowest attendance:	7,076 v Luton
Average attendance:	9,547
Total sendings-off:	7
Total bookings:	74

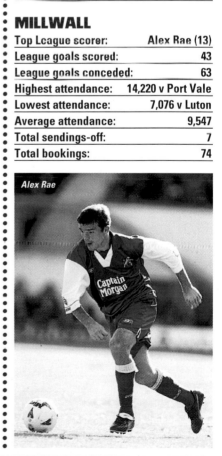

Alex Rae

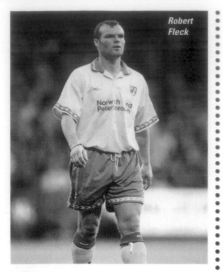
Robert Fleck

NORWICH

Top League scorer:	Robert Fleck,
	Ashley Ward (10)
League goals scored:	59
League goals conceded:	55
Highest attendance:	18,435 v Leicester
Lowest attendance:	10,945 v Sheff Utd
Average attendance:	14,580
Total sendings-off:	4
Total bookings:	56

OLDHAM

Top League scorer:	Lee Richardson (11)
League goals scored:	54
League goals conceded:	50
Highest attendance:	10,271 v Stoke
Lowest attendance:	4,225 v Tranmere
Average attendance:	6,627
Total sendings-off:	3
Total bookings:	53

PORT VALE

Top League scorer:	Tony Naylor (11)
League goals scored:	59
League goals conceded:	66
Highest attendance:	16,737 v Stoke
Lowest attendance:	5,796 v Grimsby
Average attendance:	8,217
Total sendings-off:	2
Total bookings:	57

PORTSMOUTH

Top League scorer:	Paul Hall,
	Alan McLoughlin (10)
League goals scored:	61
League goals conceded:	69
Highest attendance:	14,434 v Derby
Lowest attendance:	6,002 v Oldham
Average attendance:	9,407
Total sendings-off:	6
Total bookings:	75

READING

Top League scorer:	Jimmy Quinn (11)
League goals scored:	54
League goals conceded:	63
Highest attendance:	12,828 v Wolves
Lowest attendance:	5,321 v Southend
Average attendance:	8,917
Total sendings-off:	1
Total bookings:	59

SHEFF UTD

Top League scorer:	Nathan Blake (12)
League goals scored:	57
League goals conceded:	54
Highest attendance:	20,050 v Sunderland
Lowest attendance:	9,448 v Charlton
Average attendance:	12,894
Total sendings-off:	4
Total bookings:	71

SOUTHEND

Top League scorer:	Dave Regis (8)
League goals scored:	52
League goals conceded:	61
Highest attendance:	8,363 v Ipswich
Lowest attendance:	4,506 v Port Vale
Average attendance:	5,915
Total sendings-off:	2
Total bookings:	55

SUNDERLAND

Top League scorer:	Craig Russell (13)
League goals scored:	59
League goals conceded:	33
Highest attendance:	22,027 v West Brom
Lowest attendance:	12,282 v Portsmouth
Average attendance:	17,503
Total sendings-off:	3
Total bookings:	44

Craig Russell

Mike Sheron

STOKE

Top League scorer:	Mike Sheron (15)
League goals scored:	60
League goals conceded:	49
Highest attendance:	18,897 v Southend
Lowest attendance:	8,618 v Tranmere
Average attendance:	12,281
Total sendings-off:	1
Total bookings:	53

TRANMERE

Top League scorer:	John Aldridge (27)
League goals scored:	64
League goals conceded:	60
Highest attendance:	16,193 v Sunderland
Lowest attendance:	5,253 v C.Palace
Average attendance:	7,861
Total sendings-off:	2
Total bookings:	55

WATFORD

Top League scorer:	Craig Ramage (15)
League goals scored:	62
League goals conceded:	70
Highest attendance:	20,089 v Leicester
Lowest attendance:	7,091 v Southend
Average attendance:	9,456
Total sendings-off:	0
Total bookings:	61

WEST BROM

Top League scorer:	Bob Taylor (17)
League goals scored:	60
League goals conceded:	68
Highest attendance:	23,858 v Derby
Lowest attendance:	10,959 v Oldham

Average attendance:	15,161
Total sendings-off:	0
Total bookings:	54

WOLVES

Top League scorer:	Don Goodman (16)
League goals scored:	56
League goals conceded:	62
Highest attendance:	28,687 v Ipswich
Lowest attendance:	20,450 v Charlton
Average attendance:	25,125
Total sendings-off:	3
Total bookings:	45

ENDSLEIGH SECOND DIVISION

BLACKPOOL

Top League scorer:	Tony Ellis, Andy Preece (14)
League goals scored:	67
League goals conceded:	40
Highest attendance:	9,175 v Swindon
Lowest attendance:	3,877 v Bristol Rvs
Average attendance:	5,817
Total sendings-off:	1
Total bookings:	66

Andy Preece

BOURNEMOUTH

Top League scorer:	Steve Jones (17)
League goals scored:	51
League goals conceded:	70
Highest attendance:	6,310 v Swindon
Lowest attendance:	3,191 v Notts Co
Average attendance:	4,211
Total sendings-off:	5
Total bookings:	49

BRADFORD

Top League scorer:	Mark Stallard (9)
League goals scored:	71
League goals conceded:	69
Highest attendance:	9,748 v Wycombe
Lowest attendance:	3,622 v Notts Co
Average attendance:	5,680
Total sendings-off:	2
Total bookings:	64

Robert Taylor

BRENTFORD

Top League scorer:	Robert Taylor (11)
League goals scored:	43
League goals conceded:	49
Highest attendance:	7,878 v Swindon
Lowest attendance:	3,104 v Carlisle
Average attendance:	4,805
Total sendings-off:	4
Total bookings:	63

BRIGHTON

Top League scorer:	Jeff Minton (8)
League goals scored:	46
League goals conceded:	69
Highest attendance:	7,808 v Swindon
Lowest attendance:	2,106 v York
Average attendance:	5,256
Total sendings-off:	3
Total bookings:	53

BRISTOL CITY

Top League scorer:	Paul Agostino, David Seal (10)
League goals scored:	55
League goals conceded:	60
Highest attendance:	20,007 v Bristol Rvs
Lowest attendance:	4,408 v Chesterfield
Average attendance:	7,039
Total sendings-off:	2
Total bookings:	35

BRISTOL RVS

Top League scorer:	Marcus Stewart (21)
League goals scored:	57
League goals conceded:	60
Highest attendance:	8,648 v Bristol City
Lowest attendance:	`3,515 v Chesterfield
Average attendance:	5,284
Total sendings-off:	2
Total bookings:	42

BURNLEY

Top League scorer:	Kurt Nogan (20)
League goals scored:	56
League goals conceded:	68
Highest attendance:	10,613 v Hull
Lowest attendance:	6,815 v Oxford
Average attendance:	9,055
Total sendings-off:	6
Total bookings:	57

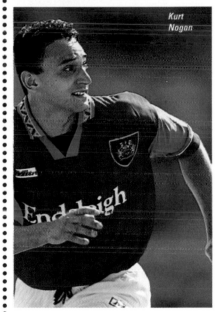

Kurt Nogan

CARLISLE

Top League scorer:	David Reeves (13)
League goals scored:	57
League goals conceded:	72
Highest attendance:	8,003 v Bristol Rvs
Lowest attendance:	3,760 v Shrewsbury
Average attendance:	5,704
Total sendings-off:	5
Total bookings:	60

CHESTERFIELD

Top League scorer:	Tony Lormor (13)
League goals scored:	56
League goals conceded:	51
Highest attendance:	7,002 v Blackpool
Lowest attendance:	3,419 v York
Average attendance:	4,884
Total sendings-off:	3
Total bookings:	43

CREWE

Top League scorer:	Rob Edwards (15)
League goals scored:	77
League goals conceded:	60
Highest attendance:	5,177 v Wrexham
Lowest attendance:	2,977 v Bristol City
Average attendance:	3,973
Total sendings-off:	1
Total bookings:	30

HULL

Top League scorer:	Richard Peacock (7)
League goals scored:	36
League goals conceded:	78
Highest attendance:	8,965 v Bradford
Lowest attendance:	2,284 v Brentford
Average attendance:	3,803
Total sendings-off:	4
Total bookings:	61

Devon White

NOTTS CO

Top League scorer:	Devon White (8)
League goals scored:	63
League goals conceded:	39
Highest attendance:	8,725 v Swindon
Lowest attendance: 3,462 v York	
Average attendance:	5,131
Total sendings-off:	2
Total bookings:	60

OXFORD

Top League scorer:	Paul Moody (17)
League goals scored:	76
League goals conceded:	39
Highest attendance:	8,585 v Swindon
Lowest attendance:	4,271 v Rotherham
Average attendance:	5,866
Total sendings-off:	2
Total bookings:	40

PETERBOROUGH

Top League scorer:	Gary Martindale (15)
League goals scored:	59
League goals conceded:	66
Highest attendance:	6,649 v Hull
Lowest attendance:	3,267 v Stockport
Average attendance:	4,655
Total sendings-off:	4
Total bookings:	59

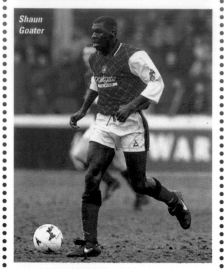

Shaun Goater

ROTHERHAM

Top League scorer:	Shaun Goater (18)
League goals scored:	54
League goals conceded:	62
Highest attendance:	6,920 v Stockport
Lowest attendance:	2,092 v Bournemouth
Average attendance:	3,422
Total sendings-off:	3
Total bookings:	63

SHREWSBURY

Top League scorer:	Ian Stevens (12)
League goals scored:	58
League goals conceded:	70
Highest attendance:	6,532 v Swansea
Lowest attendance:	2,186 v Oxford
Average attendance:	3,317
Total sendings-off:	4
Total bookings:	53

STOCKPORT

Top League scorer:	Alun Armstrong (13)
League goals scored:	61
League goals conceded:	47
Highest attendance:	8,463 v Burnley
Lowest attendance:	3,731 v Bristol City
Average attendance:	5,902
Total sendings-off:	0
Total bookings:	43

SWANSEA

Top League scorer:	Steve Torpey (15)

League goals scored:	43
League goals conceded:	79
Highest attendance:	4,478 v Blackpool
Lowest attendance:	1,788 v Rotherham
Average attendance:	2,974
Total sendings-off:	1
Total bookings:	64

SWINDON

Top League scorer:	Wayne Allison (17)
League goals scored:	71
League goals conceded:	34
Highest attendance:	14,697 v Stockport
Lowest attendance:	6,555 v Swansea
Average attendance:	10,039
Total sendings-off:	0
Total bookings:	38

WALSALL

Top League scorer:	Kevin Wilson, Kyle Lightbourne (15)
League goals scored:	60
League goals conceded:	45
Highest attendance:	5,624 v Swindon
Lowest attendance:	2,752 v Hull
Average attendance:	3,982
Total sendings-off:	3
Total bookings:	30

WREXHAM

Top League scorer:	Karl Connolly (18)
League goals scored:	76
League goals conceded:	55
Highest attendance:	6,664 v Burnley
Lowest attendance:	2,004 v Bournemouth
Average attendance:	3,692
Total sendings-off:	4
Total bookings:	53

WYCOMBE

Top League scorer:	Miguel Desouza (18)
League goals scored:	63
League goals conceded:	59
Highest attendance:	6,727 v Oxford
Lowest attendance:	2,936 v Rotherham
Average attendance:	4,580
Total sendings-off:	6
Total bookings:	45

YORK

Top League scorer:	Paul Barnes (15)
League goals scored:	58
League goals conceded:	73
Highest attendance:	7,147 v Blackpool
Lowest attendance:	2,055 v Bournemouth
Average attendance:	3,537
Total sendings-off:	1
Total bookings:	50

ENDSLEIGH THIRD DIVISION

BARNET

Top League scorer:	Sean Devine (19)
League goals scored:	65
League goals conceded:	45
Highest attendance:	4,332 v Fulham
Lowest attendance:	1,674 v Scunthorpe
Average attendance:	2,281
Total sendings-off:	2
Total bookings:	53

BURY

Top League scorer:	Mark Carter (16)
League goals scored:	66
League goals conceded:	48
Highest attendance:	5,658 v Cardiff
Lowest attendance:	2,280 v Hereford
Average attendance:	3,261
Total sendings-off:	6
Total bookings:	46

CAMBRIDGE

Top League scorer:	Carlo Corazzin,
	Steve Butler (10)
League goals scored:	61
League goals conceded:	71
Highest attendance:	4,114 v Gillingham
Lowest attendance:	2,186 v Rochdale
Average attendance:	2,766
Total sendings-off:	5
Total bookings:	56

CARDIFF

Top League scorer:	Carl Dale (21)
League goals scored:	41
League goals conceded:	64
Highest attendance:	7,872 v Northampton
Lowest attendance:	1,612 v Wigan
Average attendance:	3,294
Total sendings-off:	4
Total bookings:	40

Carl Dale

CHESTER

Top League scorer:	Stuart Rimmer,
	Chris Priest (13)
League goals scored:	72
League goals conceded:	53
Highest attendance:	5,004 v Preston
Lowest attendance:	1,623 v Cambridge
Average attendance:	2,699
Total sendings-off:	4
Total bookings:	49

COLCHESTER

Top League scorer:	Tony Adcock (12)
League goals scored:	61
League goals conceded:	51
Highest attendance:	5,038 v Doncaster
Lowest attendance:	2,138 v Scunthorpe
Average attendance:	3,274
Total sendings-off:	7
Total bookings:	63

Tony Adcock

DARLINGTON

Top League scorer:	Robert Blake (11)
League goals scored:	60
League goals conceded:	42
Highest attendance:	4,510 v Chester
Lowest attendance:	1,502 v Doncaster
Average attendance:	2,396
Total sendings-off:	2
Total bookings:	52

DONCASTER

Top League scorer:	Graeme Jones (10)
League goals scored:	49
League goals conceded:	60
Highest attendance:	4,413 v Preston
Lowest attendance:	1,429 v Exeter
Average attendance:	2,090
Total sendings-off:	6
Total bookings:	53

EXETER

Top League scorer:	David Cooper (6)
League goals scored:	46
League goals conceded:	53
Highest attendance:	6,185 v Plymouth
Lowest attendance:	2,439 v Scarborough
Average attendance:	3,440
Total sendings-off:	3
Total bookings:	41

Mike Conroy

FULHAM

Top League scorer:	Mike Conroy (9)
League goals scored:	57
League goals conceded:	63
Highest attendance:	10,320 v Gillingham
Lowest attendance:	2,176 v Scunthorpe
Average attendance:	4,183
Total sendings-off:	4
Total bookings:	47

GILLINGHAM

Top League scorer:	Leo F'tune-West (12)
League goals scored:	49
League goals conceded:	20
Highest attendance:	10,602 v Preston
Lowest attendance:	3,901 v Wigan
Average attendance:	7,203
Total sendings-off:	5
Total bookings:	80

HARTLEPOOL

Top League scorer:	Joe Allon (8)
League goals scored:	47
League goals conceded:	67
Highest attendance:	5,076 v Preston
Lowest attendance:	1,198 v Fulham
Average attendance:	2,113
Total sendings-off:	9
Total bookings:	60

HEREFORD

Top League scorer:	Steve White (29)
League goals scored:	65
League goals conceded:	47
Highest attendance:	5,880 v Rochdale
Lowest attendance:	1,631 v Lincoln
Average attendance:	2,971
Total sendings-off:	3
Total bookings:	46

L. ORIENT

Top League scorer:	Colin West (16)
League goals scored:	44
League goals conceded:	62
Highest attendance:	8,221 v Torquay
Lowest attendance:	2,121 v Scarborough
Average attendance:	4,494
Total sendings-off:	4
Total bookings:	49

LINCOLN

Top League scorer:	Gareth Ainsw'th (12)
League goals scored:	57
League goals conceded:	73
Highest attendance:	5,814 v Torquay
Lowest attendance:	1,841 v L.Orient
Average attendance:	3,000
Total sendings-off:	2
Total bookings:	74

Gareth Ainsworth

MANSFIELD

Top League scorer:	Stewart Hadley, Mark Sale (7)
League goals scored:	54
League goals conceded:	64
Highest attendance:	4,661 v Preston
Lowest attendance:	1,674 v Torquay
Average attendance:	2,416
Total sendings-off:	5
Total bookings:	55

NORTHAMPTON

Top League scorer:	Jason White (16)
League goals scored:	51
League goals conceded:	44
Highest attendance:	7,427 v Gillingham
Lowest attendance:	3,090 v Rochdale
Average attendance:	4,830
Total sendings-off:	4
Total bookings:	60

PLYMOUTH

Top League scorer:	Adrian Littlejohn (17)
League goals scored:	68
League goals conceded:	49
Highest attendance:	12,427 v Exeter
Lowest attendance:	4,536 v Bury
Average attendance:	7,132
Total sendings-off:	3
Total bookings:	52

Andy Saville

PRESTON

Top League scorer:	Andy Saville (29)
League goals scored:	78
League goals conceded:	38
Highest attendance:	18,700 v Exeter
Lowest attendance:	6,837 v Wigan
Average attendance:	9,999
Total sendings-off:	2
Total bookings:	34

ROCHDALE

Top League scorer:	Steve Whitehall (20)
League goals scored:	57
League goals conceded:	61
Highest attendance:	4,597 v Preston
Lowest attendance:	1,206 v Torquay
Average attendance:	2,213
Total sendings-off:	3

Total bookings:	57

SCARBOROUGH

Top League scorer:	Andy Ritchie (8)
League goals scored:	39
League goals conceded:	69
Highest attendance:	3,771 v Preston
Lowest attendance:	1,201 v Colchester
Average attendance:	1,713
Total sendings-off:	3
Total bookings:	43

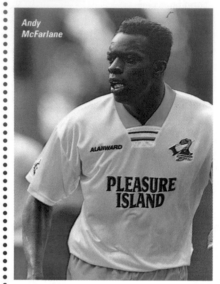

Andy McFarlane

SCUNTHORPE

Top League scorer:	Andy McFarlane (16)
League goals scored:	67
League goals conceded:	61
Highest attendance:	4,847 v Darlington
Lowest attendance:	1,615 v Exeter
Average attendance:	2,434
Total sendings-off:	2
Total bookings:	40

TORQUAY

Top League scorer:	Paul Baker (5)
League goals scored:	30
League goals conceded:	84
Highest attendance:	4,269 v Plymouth
Lowest attendance:	1,456 v Bury
Average attendance:	2,438
Total sendings-off:	2
Total bookings:	58

WIGAN

Top League scorer:	Isdro Diaz (10)
League goals scored:	62
League goals conceded:	56
Highest attendance:	5,567 v Preston
Lowest attendance:	1,745 v Barnet
Average attendance:	2,855
Total sendings-off:	4
Total bookings:	44

INTERNATIONAL RESCUE
New bosses have to rebuild

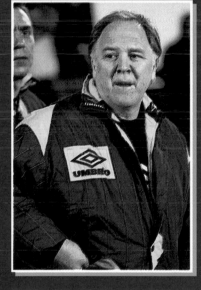

WELCOME to our monster eleven-page international section, where we bring you all the stars from England, Scotland, Wales, and the two Irelands.

All five teams are currently in a transitional period with dozens of young players coming to the fore.

Glenn Hoddle has the pick of the bunch with top stars from Liverpool and Manchester United already cherishing silverware and having years of international fame ahead of them.

Craig Brown is trying to turn a capable Scotland side into a top class one, but struggles when his top stars are out.

But at least he has loads of Premier players to choose from. Bobby Gould, Bryan Hamilton and Mick McCarthy have to delve into reserve teams, the Endsleigh League and their own domestic part-time football to search for rough diamonds.

All three managers know they have to get the kids in the team early and try to polish them into little gems, and with the help of the senior stars, they could keep their hats in the ring for a place in the World Cup Finals.

Qualification is under way already, so stay tuned......

GLENN'S GLEE

GLENN HODDLE takes over as England boss for the World Cup qualifiers in the Autumn of 1996, knowing that he has a team capable of sticking together for the next five years. Terry Venables may have retained half of the squad he inherited from Graham Taylor but he has added an exciting group of youngsters who have come up through the Under-21 team.

The Nevilles in defence, Jamie Redknapp, Steve McManaman and Darren Anderton in midfield, and Robbie Fowler up front should all form the basis of Hoddle's new England squad.

Veterans Stuart Pearce, David Platt and Peter Beardsley could have reached the end of their international careers but there are players ready to take their places.

Steve Stone, Steve Howey, Stan Collymore and Rob Lee have all made an impact on the side in 1996 and, with England having to win competitive games for the first time in nearly three years, qualification for World Cup '98 will rest heavily on the shoulders of this new England side.

And there will be more to come - Hoddle wants United stars David Beckham, Nicky Butt and Paul Scholes to step up from the Under-21s to take England all the way to the finals in Paris.

Hoddle's delighted to reign England

NEW FACES

ROBBIE FOWLER
His goals record spoke for itself but Terry Venables made him wait until March 1996 before putting him in the England squad - then the Liverpool striker was not left in the stands, but handed the first of what should be many England caps. He ended a run of goals on intenrational debuts, but secured his place in the squad for Euro 96 and should play a major part in Glenn Hoddle's plans for World Cup '98.

PHIL NEVILLE
Big brother Gary took six months to go from his Premiership debut into the England squad. Phil took ten but, by the end of 1995-96, he was more likely to be in the Manchester United starting line-up than Gary. A former England schoolboy international at both cricket and football, Phil showed he could play at left-back or right-back and with so much international expereince behind him, nothing seemd to worry him as he won a Championship medal aged only 19.

GARETH SOUTHGATE
In his early 20s Gareth was captain of Crystal Palace but he couldn't stop them dropping out of the Premiership only a year after bouncing back up. A £2.5m move to Aston Villa in the summer of 1995 enabled Southgate to show he was international class with some inspired performances in defence for Villa. Terry Venables already knew what he could do in midfield and his versatility earned him a place in the England squad.

1995-96 Results

September 6	England 0	Colombia 0
October 11	Norway 0	England 0
November 15	England 3	Switzerland 1
	Pearce, Sheringham, Stone	
December 12	England 1	Portugal 1
	Stone	
March 27	England 1	Bulgaria 0
	Ferdinand	
April 24	England 0	Croatia 0
(All matches are friendlies.)		

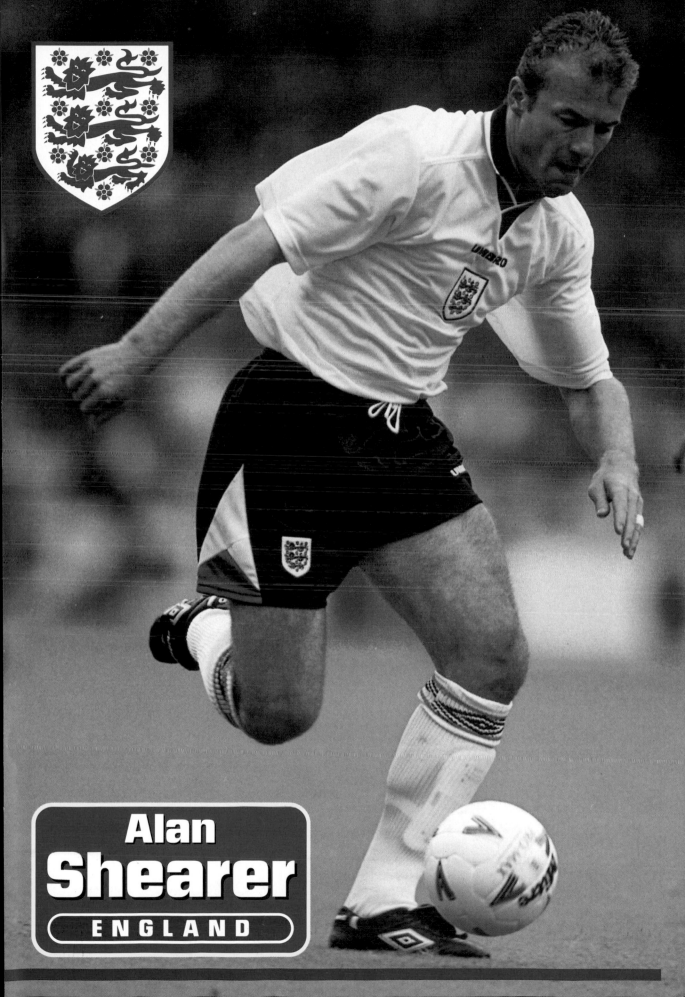

Alan Shearer
ENGLAND

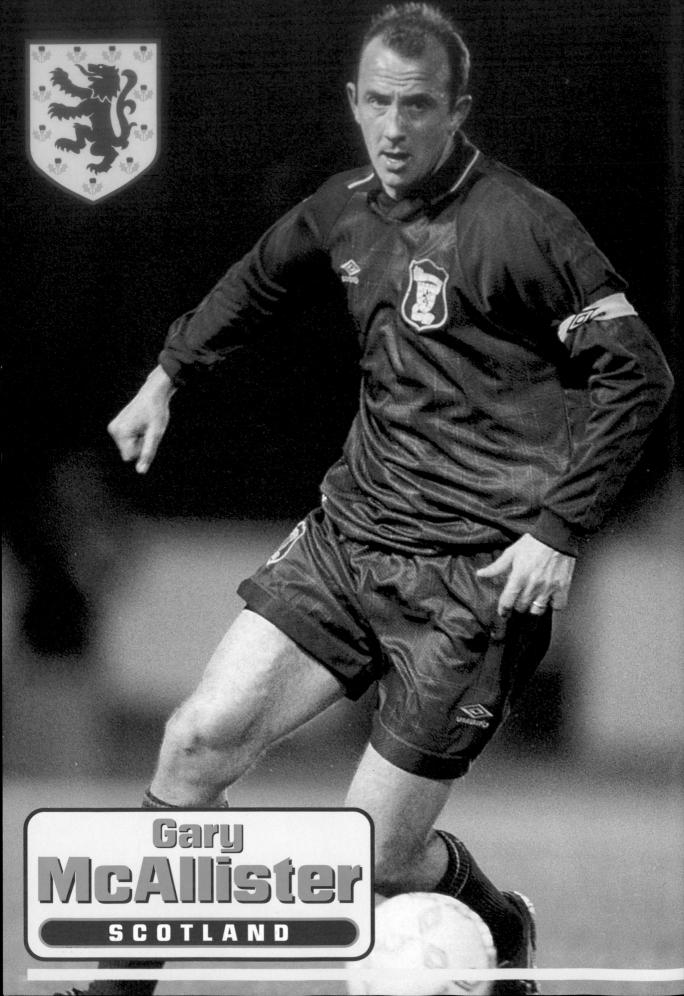

Gary McAllister

SCOTLAND

SHUT THAT DOOR
Scotland put defences first

AFTER CRAIG Brown's side qualified for Euro 96 with a fantastic defensive record, he had to work out how they were going to start scoring.

He tried plenty of options; John Spencer, Kevin Gallacher, Duncan Shearer, Darren Jackson, Scott Booth, Eoin Jess, Gordon Durie - the list is virtually endless. But after all the experiments, the one man who came like cream to the top of the milk, was Ally McCoist.

He celebrated his 50th cap with the only goal in the win over Australia, and showed that he has plenty left in him, despite being 34 at the start of the 1996-97 season.

With a midfield featuring Gary McAllister, John Collins and Stuart McCall, there is no lack of class in that department, and with the likes of Colin Hendry and Celtic's rising star Jackie McNamara in defence, the Scots are putting together a strong looking side.

And there are also some exciting youngsters looking to establish themselves as first choices, like these three...

NEW FACES

SCOTT GEMMILL
The son of former Forest and Scotland star Archie, Scott won his first Scotland caps in 1995, and his performances in Forest's midfield have secured his place in the full squad after several games at Under-21 and B level.

A tough tackler but confident threading through balls to the strikers, Scott (above) is a versatile player who could well earn as many as his dad's 43 caps.

CRAIG BURLEY
Another young player with a famous relative, Craig is well on the way to matching the 11 caps his Uncle George won for Scotland before going into management.

Craig (left) developed considerably as a versatile midfielder under Glenn Hoddle at Chelsea, and he has established himself as quiet, assured presence in the Scotland side.

Ruud Gullit's influence can't be overlooked either as the Ayr-born star progressed to the full Scotland squad - the fourth level he has won caps at.

EOIN JESS
Coventry playmaker Jess had Paul McStay to thank for his place at last summer's Euro 96 tournament, but now he looks set to make one of the midfield berths his own.

Jess (above) had to cancel his holiday in the Carribbean to line up in the summer when McStay was ruled out with a knee injury, and he is certain to be a key figure in the qualification campaign for the 1998 World Cup finals in France.

Playing in England should make him a better player and if he shows the form he did for Aberdeen, he could become one of the Premier's top stars.

1995-96 Results
October 11 Sweden 2 Scotland 0
March 27   Scotland 1 Australia 0 (McCoist)
April 24   Denmark 2 Scotland 0
(All matches are friendlies.)

THE GOULD-EN BOYS

Wales turn to the kids

WHEN BOBBY GOULD took over the Welsh manager's job last season, he knew he had to start again, almost from scratch.

They had failed time and time again to qualify for major tournaments, and Neville Southall and Ian Rush were coming to the end of their international playing careers.

So without writing them off completely, he asked both top stars to help him coach the new squad, and set about 'doing a Jack Charlton'. That is, recruiting as many young, promising players who are qualified by any means to play for Wales as he can.

While the likes of Ryan Giggs, Mark Hughes, Southall and Rush were all rested, Gould threw new faces into the fray.

Goalkeeper Tommy Coyne, Christian Edwards, John Robinson, Andy Legg and Gareth Taylor, Simon Davies, Andy Marriott and Rob Savage were all given a taste of international football before their opening World Cup '98 qualifiers.

Hughes and Giggs will return to give some experience to the side with Vinny Jones, Chris Coleman, Barry Horne, Mark Pembridge and John Hartson the only other regular Premiership players available.

It's not a huge pool of talent but Gould knows he must get more from them than his predecessors.

NEW FACES

ANDY MARRIOTT

A bizarre recruitment by Bobby Gould, goalkeeper Marriott was born and bred in Nottingham and played for England at Under-15, Youth and Under-21 level while a reserve at Arsenal and Nottingham Forest.

He moved to Wrexham three years ago and won over the Welsh fans with some stunning performances.

Gould discovered that Marriott had Welsh ancestors and suddenly he was thrown into the squad and immediately made his debut against Switzerland. He will compete with Tranmere's Tommy Coyne to become Neville Southall's replacement in Wales' goal for years to come.

SIMON DAVIES

Ironically, Davies came to light playing for Manchester United in the Champions League, mainly because he was English!

He was in and out of the United side in 1994-95 but fell out of favour with Alex Ferguson last season and was leapfrogged by David Beckham in the pecking order for wide midfielders at Old Trafford.

Already 22, Davies is expected to leave United this season but his performances for their Championsip-winning reserve side impressed Gould enough to draft him into the Welsh squad thanks to his family's Welsh roots.

He made his debut as a sub in Switzerland and will be part of the new Wales squad.

ROB SAVAGE

Another former United trainee, Savage also made his debut in Switzerland and his confident runs showed no signs of nerves.

Born in Wrexham in 1974, Savage left Old Trafford in 1994 without making a first team appearence.

He joined Crewe but still failed

to convince Dario Gradi he was worth a regular place until he turned on the style last season.

Bobby Gould liked what he saw and blooded the blond attacker in the new-look Wales side that went down 2-1 in Switzerland.

1995-96 Results		
October 11*	Wales 1	Germany 2
	Helmer og	
January 24	Italy 3	Wales 0
April 24	Switzerland 2	Wales 0
*(All matches friendlies except * indicates Euro 96 qualifier.)*		

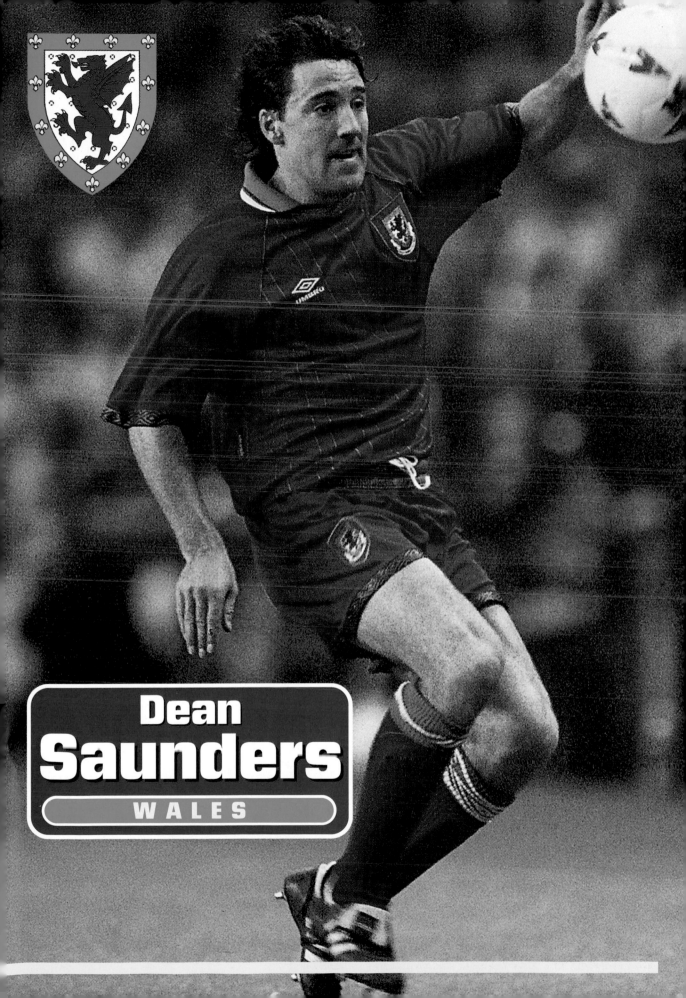

Dean Saunders

WALES

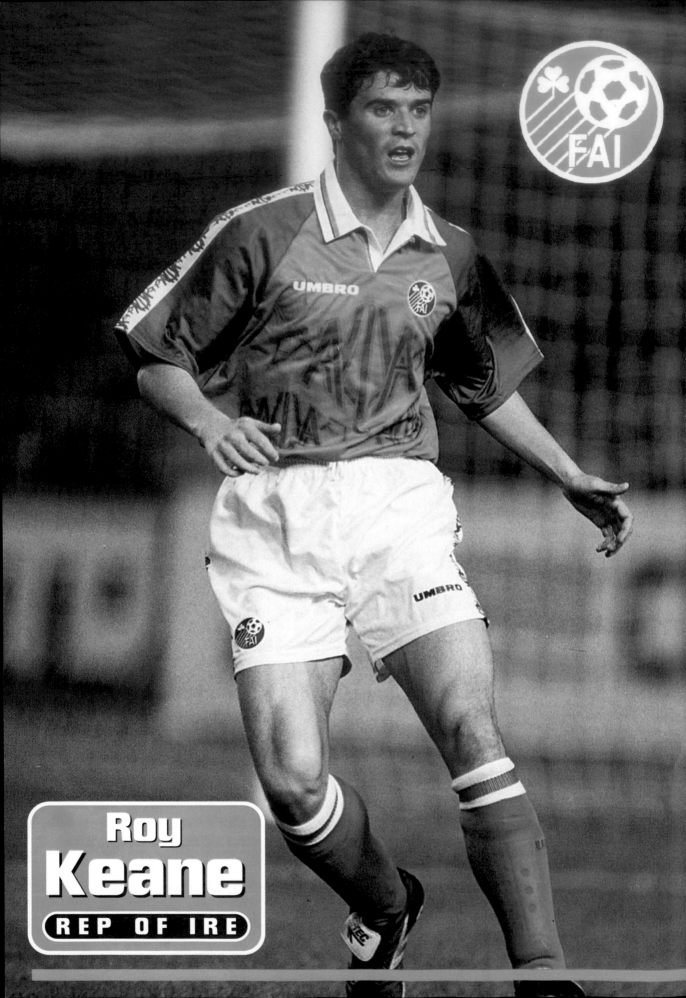

FAI

Roy Keane
REP OF IRE

BIG MICK'S MIX

McCarthy throws together vets and kids

NEW FACES

RATHER THAN send a whole regiment of untested new boys straight into international action, like Bobby Gould did with Wales, Mick McCarthy retained the services of Jack Charlton's veterans when he became Republic boss last season.

The former Millwall manager decided his best bet was to keep the likes of Paul McGrath, Steve Staunton, Ray Houghton, Niall Quinn and Tony Cascarino.

But he had little choice. With a string of friendlies against Russia, the Czechs, Portugal, Croatia and Holland, Ireland were competing in their own mini European Championship.

Little by little, McCarthy is bringing in players who will be at their peak in two years time when the World Cup comes to a climax.

But the lack of quality strikers is a worry for McCarthy. Although John Aldridge's goals keep flowing, together, Aldo, Quinn and Cascarino are 99-years-old!

So McCarthy has been very brave. He's taken left-winger Mark Kennedy from Liverpool reserves and put him up front for Ireland, with 19-year-old David Connolly zooming straight into the full squad after a burst of goals for Watford.

SHAY GIVEN

With Alan Kelly injured, Blackburn's Shay Given was handed his first chance against Russia in March 1996 - three weeks before his 20th birthday!

The teenager (left) earned his cap not by playing for the ex-Premiership Champions, but for the First Division title-winners, Sunderland.

When Shay went on loan, Sunderland were tenth. When he returned to Ewood Park, they were five points clear at the top!

Given kept twelve clean sheets in his 17 appearances but is still unlikely to dislodge Tim Flowers from Blackburn's goal this season.

LIAM DAISH

A Portsmouth lad, Daish made only one appearence for his home town team before moving to John Beck's Cambridge. He took them to the verge of the Premiership and on two FA Cup runs, and that form earned him a move to

Birmingham three years ago.

The giant centre-half (above) was Barry Fry's favourite but he snapped up Coventry's £1.5m bid for Daish in February 1996.

The 28-year-old defender is seen as a direct replacement for Paul McGrath and should add to his Under-21 and B call-ups with many full caps.

ALAN MOORE

A true Dubliner, Moore has been at Middlesbrough for five years and was a vital part of their team that reached the Premiership. But the 21-year-old left-winger s truggled to hold down a regular place in Bryan Robson's starting line-up last season.

However, he did enough to show he could cope with international football and was called-up from the Republic's Under-21 squad to play the whole game against the Czech Republic last April.

1995-96 Results		
October 11*	Rep of Ire 2	Latvia 1
	Aldridge 2	
December 13*P/O	Rep of Ire 0	Holland 2
March 27	Rep ofIre 0	Russia 2
April 24	Czech Rep 2	Rep of Ire 0
*(All matches friendlies except * indicates Euro 96 qualifier.)*		

IRISH AHOY

Hammo's men creep up on the rails

OUT OF THE RACE to qualify for the last two major tournaments, Bryan Hamilton has been slowly rebuilding a Northern Ireland side that spent the first half of the 90s struggling to match the achievements of the 80s.

But while the world's media ignored them, Northern Ireland have quietly turned things around and would have pipped the Republic to their Play-Off place with Holland if Euro 96 qualification rules had been the same as in the Premiership.

A win in Austria and a draw in Portugal showed the potential of this improving side - only the defeats at home to the Republic and in Latvia wrecked any chance of making it to the finals.

Hamilton organised a string of tough friendlies against the likes of Norway and Sweden to get newcomers like Spurs' Gerry McMahon, Blackpool's James Quinn, and Port Vale winger Jon McCarthy ready for qualifiers against Germany and Portugal.

Hamilton's men will have to gather up almost maximum points off Armenia, Albania and Ukraine if they are going to pip either Portugal or Germany to a ticket to France 98.

He's playing it down, but Hamilton knows that with the likes of Newcastle star Keith Gillespie and Leicester's Neil Lennon, anything's possible.

NEW FACES

DARREN PATTERSON

An important member of the Crystal Palace side that won promotion to the Premiership in 1994, Patterson (left) is a strong centre-half who has rescued his career at Luton after missing two seasons with injury and loss of form. Born in Belfast, Patterson went to West Brom as a youngster but joined Wigan where he played nearly 100 times. The move to Palace was a flop until 1994-5 when he got in the first team and won his first cap. Now he's doing the business for both Luton and Ireland.

KEITH ROWLAND

Signed from Bournemouth for £110,000 in 1993 after a loan spell to Coventry failed to work out, Keith has Slaven Bilic to thank for his place in West Ham's starting line-up. Once the Crotian arrived, Harry Redknapp played a 3-5-2 formation, with Julian Dicks alongside Bilic at the back. That gave Rowland (left) a chance as a left wing-back and he has grabbed it. Likely to be a permanent member of Bryan Hamilton's side this season, Rowland looks to be fulfilling his potential at last.

GERRY MCMAHON

Another Northern Ireland regular who is frustrated by a lack of first team opportunities in the Premiership, McMahon spent most of last season on the Spurs' bench. The 22-year-old midfielder (below) is the spitting image of Steve McManaman and plays a similar role to the roving winger. He impressed on loan at Barnet in 1994-5 and won his first cap on the tour of Canada that summer, and is now being used as well as Keith Gillespie, rather than as his replacement on the right of midfield.

1995-96 Results

October 11*	Leichtenstein 0	N.Ireland 4
		O'Neil, McMahon, Quinn, Gray
March 27	N.Ireland 0	Norway 2
April 24	N.Ireland 1	Sweden 2
	McMahon	

*(All matches friendlies except *indicates Euro 96 qualifier.)*

Keith Gillespie

N. IRELAND

Steve Stone
NOTTM FOR

KING KINKY

BEASANT

KINKLADZE

KINKLADZE

SHIPPERLEY

SHIPPERLEY

MONKOU

KINKLADZE

CHARLTON

KINKLADZE

LOMAS

CLOUGH

Georgiou Kinkladze
Man City v Southampton
Date: March 16
Venue: Maine Road

Manchester City didn't have much to smile about last year, but they did unearth one of the jewels of the season.

Georgiou Kinkladze lit up the Premiership with his dazzling footwork, magical left foot and blinding goals.

And the midfield maestro produced one of the best strikes ever seen at Maine Road when he helped City to a 2-1 win Southampton.

Kinky had already given City the lead with an early goal, but there seemed little danger when he picked up the ball just in Saints' half.

But then the little Georgian international started to weave his magic wand, or rather his spell binding left foot, as he carved his way past four Southampton defenders and then cooly chipped the ball over the advancing 'keeper Dave Beasant.

It brought Maine Road to its feet and even Saints' own goal magician, Matt Le Tissier, applauded a strike he would have been proud of.

RETURN OF THE RED

Eric Cantona
Man Utd v Wimbledon
Date: February 3
Venue: Selhurst Park

The eyes of the soccer world were on Eric Cantona when he returned to Selhurst Park for a Premiership clash with Wimbledon.

The South London ground was the scene of one of the most controversial incidents in the game, and the most infamous in British football history.

A year before United's clash with The Dons, Cantona had been sent-off in a League game at Selhurst against Crystal Palace.

A minute after the red card, he launched a kung-fu kick at a Palace supporter. A ten-month ban from football followed for the wayward genius, not to mention an initial two-week prison sentence.

But the Frenchman returned to football a changed man and showed all his skills when United triumphed 4-2 at Wimbledon.

This goal illustrated all the good things in his play. After an intricate passing move, he left The Dons defence trailing to spread the ball out to young flyer, David Beckham.

The Reds midfielder crossed and Cantona headed superbly past Neil Sullivan to set United on the way to three vital points.

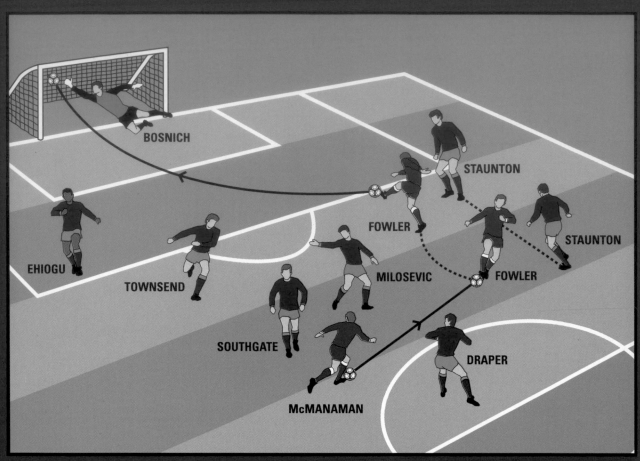

FOWLER POWER

Robbie Fowler
Liverpool v Aston Villa
Date: March 3
Venue: Anfield

Aston Villa arrived at Anfield for a crucial Championship clash with both sides still in the hunt for glory.

Five minutes into the game the visitors were down and out, left shattered by a breathtaking blitz from The Reds, and Robbie Fowler in particular.

The England star left Villa in tatters with two superb goals, one a spectacular long range effort that left highly-rated Aussie 'keeper Mark Bosnich stunned.

Fowler picked the ball up 35 yards from goal, left his marker bamboozled with a twist and turn and then thundered a shot past the bemused Bosnich.

"It was a wonderful strike and there was no way I could get near it," said Mark.

"Fowler was in brilliant form and Liverpool pulverised us in that opening few minutes. We just couldn't recover."

WRIGHT AHEAD

Ian Wright
Arsenal v Newcastle
Date: January 10
Venue: Highbury

Newcastle arrived at Highbury for this Coca-Cola Cup Quarter-Final clash with The Gunners full of confidence after a Fourth Round win at Liverpool and dreaming of their first Wembley visit in 21 years.

They left beaten and battered by the brilliance of Ian Wright.

The England international tormented Kevin Keegan's side all night and it was his two strikes that tipped the balance The Gunners' way.

The first goal was the pick of the two and had the North Bank faithful on their feet.

Wrighty received the ball on the right side of the Newcastle box, jinked past the Geordie defenders and unleashed a thunderbolt strike that caught 'keeper Pavel Srnicek by surprise.

But what really deceived the St James' Park stopper was the swerve that Wright inflicted on the ball to send it screaming past Srnicek's outstretched hand.

It was a golden goal from a Goalden Gunner.

MACCA MAGIC

Gary McAllister
Leeds v Port Vale
Date: February 27
Venue: Vale Park

Port Vale had already ended the FA Cup hopes of holders Everton at Vale Park in the Fourth Round and they seemed set for another Premiership scalp.

Leeds were a goal down and heading out of the Cup until their captain came to the rescue again.

When his side needed him most, Gary McAllister was up to the challenge and produced two marvellous pieces of skill to guide Leeds through to the next round.

He headed the visitors level from close range after Tomas Brolin had crossed from the left and then, when Leeds were awarded a free-kick on the edge of the Vale box in the last few minutes of the game, the stage was set for a Macca special.

The Scotsman stepped up to curl an absolutely perfect free-kick around the Vale wall and into the corner of the net to give Leeds a very unlikely 2-1 win.

SAVO THE MOMENT

Savo Milosevic
Aston Villa v Leeds
Date: March 24
Venue: Wembley

Savo Milosevic saved his best performance in an Aston Villa shirt for the biggest stage of the season.

The much criticised Serb, who arrived at Villa Park in a club record £3.5 million deal in the summer of 1995, had been ridiculed for his poor showing in front of goal during the League campaign but he silenced his doubters with a Wembley wonder show in his side's 3-0 win over Leeds in the Coca-Cola Cup Final.

And Milosevic provided the brightest moment of a star-spangled performance by Brian Little's side with the opening goal that left Leeds so stunned they never recovered.

The powerful striker picked the ball up halfway into his opponents' half and broke past the retreating defenders before launching an unstoppable 25-yard bullet into the top corner of John Lukic's net.

"To score at Wembley is a dream," said Savo. "Something I will always remember as long as I live."

KAN KAN

Andrei Kanchelskis
Everton v Blackburn
Date: March 30
Venue: Ewood Park

Blackburn had one of the best home records in the League during the 1995-96 season, but they were taken apart by an Everton side led by the raiding attacks of Andrei Kanchelskis.

The flying Russian tormented the Rovers defence all afternoon and his pace and skill combined to leave Tim Flowers facing a barrage of blistering strikes from all angles.

The England international 'keeper provided heroics to keep out Kanchelskis on a number of occasions but he couldn't stop the former Manchester United star contributing two of Everton's goals in a 3-0 win.

And the final nail in Blackburn's coffin illustrated Andrei at his best - and most lethal.

His pace took him clear of the Rovers defence and into a one-on-one situation with Flowers, but the 'keeper had no answer to Kanchelskis' finish - a cool volleyed chip into the net.

The GLOBAL GAME

Football is truly a worldwide game and in this section we feature some of Europe's top stars. There's Paul Ince's warning to AC Milan, we pick out, perhaps, the six best players in Europe, there's a preview to 1998 World Cup and a tribute to the Champions of '95. So read on..

Inter Mission

INCE AND CO ARE GUNNING FOR MILAN

Serie A is widely regarded as being the best League in the world and last season provided some real thrills. AC Milan were again crowned Champions - their fourth title in five years - but one man is determined they won't retain their crown...

PAUL INCE is a man who knows what he wants.

He grew up in a tough environment in London's East End but came through that to make his name with West Ham in the mid-80s.

He then moved north, to Manchester, and helped United become the team of the 90s in England as they swept all before them.

He then swapped his success-laden lifestyle to take on a new, and probably his greatest, challenge...to make Inter Milan great again.

The Italian giants were determined to lure Ince to the land of the lira and, even after agreeing a £7 million fee with United, they were prepared to wait while Ince made up his mind.

Eventually, after much soul-searching, The Guv'nor said 'Si' and now he is determined to repay Inter for the faith they showed in him.

Ince was their best player in the second half of the season but not even he could stop their great San Siro rivals, AC, from running away with the Serie A title.

But, if the England midfield star has his way, MIlan won't have things their own way this time around.

Ince insists: "I can certainly see us being up there with Milan in the race for the title.

"We had a difficult time to start with last season as new players, myself included, took a while to settle in.

"Things weren't going to well but when Roy Hodgson was brought in as the new coach things began to improve almost straight away. Now we really feel we are getting somewhere."

And that will be a relief to Ince, who grew accustomed to winning during five glorious, trophy-filled years at Old Trafford.

And having seen that side of the coin, he knows how Inter's fans must feel when their

Scudetto Scramble

Inter won't be the only side with Milan in their sights this season. Here are a few other clubs who will fancy their chances of claiming the title...

JUVENTUS

They lost their crown to Milan last season as they concentrated all their efforts on the European Cup. But this year they will be back in the title hunt, and they certainly have the players to mount a serious challenge. Any side with attacking players of the quality of Del Piero and Ravanelli must be taken seriously.
KEY MAN: Alessandro Del Piero

FIORENTINA

Two years ago they were in Serie B, but a season in the lower league seemed to do them the world of good and they bounced back better than ever last season. For a long time they were Milan's nearest challengers, before fading near the end.
KEY MAN: Gabriel Batistuta

PARMA

Forever the bridesmaids, never the brides...that has been Parma's tale of woe for the past few years. They have been hugely successful in Cup competitions, both at home and abroad, but have not been able to show the consistency to take the title. Their fans will be praying this is their year.
KEY MAN: Gianfranco Zola

LAZIO

Now firmly established as one of Italy's top six sides, Gazza's old team are just finding that final push a little too much. On their day they are capable of beating anyone, but they are prone to drop points against sides they should beat comfortably. Like Parma, consistency is the key.
KEY MAN: Giuseppe Signori

rivals are winning things year after year.

Ince was in that position with United, while the City fans had to watch from afar.

That is the position the Inter faithful now find themselves in, and Ince admits: "Our fans are probably a bit jealous of Milan, but I do think things will get better.

"Our fans sense that we've got a chance of getting the better of Milan. They believe it, and I do, too."

EU Beauties

SHOOT spotlight on Europe's top stars

GEORGE WEAH
(AC Milan & Liberia)

Currently considered to be the world's greatest player, and who are we to argue?

The Liberian was named as European, African and World Player of the Year in 1995 - a unique treble which is almost certain never to be repeated.

And all that was achieved after being handed arguably the toughest task in football, to replace Marco Van Basten.

Weah was the man Milan turned to when Van Basten had to retire through injury and there is no greater tribute to his ability than the fact that Milan have not missed the Dutch master.

The only pity is that, as the star of a weak Liberian team, Weah is never likely to get the chance to prove his ability at the very highest level in the World Cup.

RAUL GONZALEZ BLANCO
(Real Madrid & Spain)

Spain's new golden boy and, before too long, he will be a household name over Europe.

Known simply as Raul, he has starred for Real Madrid in the past couple of seasons and, so keen are they to keep him, that the Spanish giants have handed him a ten-year mega-bucks contract.

And that just emphasises the enormous promise that the teenager first showed when he broke into the first-team picture and relegated the great Emil Butragueno to the subs' bench.

That was some build-up but Raul has taken all the pressure in his stride and, with him leading the way, Madrid could yet recapture their glory days of the 60s.

PATRICK KLUIVERT
(Ajax & Holland)

Young striker who is set to follow in the footsteps of Marco Van Basten and Ruud Gullit by becoming Holland's biggest star.

Brought up in the Ajax way, he has fantastic ball skills, but marries those with a steely determination and a sharp eye for goal.

He first came to prominence when he scored the winner for Ajax in the 1995 Champions' Cup Final against AC Milan, and he has never looked back.

And, be warned, the best is yet to come.

JURGEN KLINSMANN
(Bayern Munich & Germany)

Now widely regarded as the best striker in Europe, Klinsmann has been a success wherever he has played.

He started in Germany, conquered Italy with Inter Milan, thrilled the French at Monaco and wowed the English during a spell at Spurs.

And between times, he helped the German national squad conquer the world when they won the 1990 World Cup in Italy.

One of the game's great thinkers, he has overcome claims that is a 'diver' and a 'cheat' to firmly establish himself in world football's Hall of Fame.

YOURI DJORKAEFF
(Paris SG & France)

It says everything about the talents of Djorkaeff that he kept Eric Cantona out of the French side for the Euro 96 qualifiers.

Anyone who can do that must be some player, and that is exactly what the Paris Saint Germain striker is.

After five years at Monaco, his move to PSG 18 months ago really kickstarted his career and now he is one of France's most valuable and important players.

At 28, he is a late starter on the international scene but there appears to be no doubt that his best days are yet to come.

ALESSANDRO DEL PIERO
(Juventus & Italy)

What more can you say about a player who is considered so good that Juventus were prepared to let Roberto Baggio leave to accommodate him in the team?

That is the measure of the esteem in which Del Piero is held and there is no doubt that he is on the verge of becoming one of world football's top stars.

Similar in many ways to Baggio, he is a mazy dribbler with a fierce shot and is absolutely lethal from set pieces.

Recently signed a long-term £1 million-a-year deal with Juventus. Not bad for a 21-year-old!

World

No sooner was Euro 96 out of the way, than all eyes turned towards World Cup 98. It's non-stop on the international front these days and the nerves will be jangling as 49 European countries battle it out for the 14 available places. This is how they line-up...

GROUP THREE

Norway, Switzerland, Finland, Hungary, Azerbaijan

NOT THE STRONGEST of groups and, on paper at least, it looks as though Norway and Switzerland should have no problems in finishing as the top two. On their day, Hungary can match anyone but it should be a straight fight between the Norwegians and the Swiss.

MEN TO WATCH: Lars Bohinen (Norway), Ciriacao Sforza (Switzerland)

GROUP ONE

Denmark, Greece, Croatia, Slovenia, Bosnia

NOT A LOT is known about Slovenia or Bosnia and it is highly likely that they will be the group whipping boys, leaving Denmark, Greece and Croatia to fight it out. Croatia's side is packed with stars and they look like group winners, with the Danes coming in second.

MEN TO WATCH: Davor Suker (Croatia), Mikkel Beck (Denmark)

GROUP FOUR

Sweden, SCOTLAND, Austria, Latvia, Belarus, Estonia

SCOTLAND FACE a few trips into the unknown on their way to France, but they must fancy their chances. Neither Sweden nor Austria qualified for Euro 96 and Craig Brown's side look to have an excellent chance of qualifying once again. Sweden are the biggest threat.

MEN TO WATCH: Martin Dahlin (Sweden), Gary McAllister (Scotland), Peter Stoger (Austria)

GROUP TWO

Italy, ENGLAND, Poland, Georgia, Moldova

THEY SAY there are no such things as easy games at international level, and this group looks to prove that. Although Italy and England will start as favourites, Poland and Georgia will have something to say about it.

MEN TO WATCH: Alessandro Del Piero (Italy), Paul Gascoigne (England), Georgi Kinkladze (Georgia)

in Motion

setting sail for France?

GROUP FIVE

Russia, Bulgaria, Israel, Cyprus, Luxembourg

IT WILL BE one of the biggest surprises in World Cup history if Russia and Bulgaria don't finish as one-two in this group. The only question is which team comes out on top and the two matches between the countries will be crucial.

MEN TO WATCH: Andrei Kanchelskis (Russia), Hristo Stoichkov (Bulgaria)

GROUP EIGHT

Romania, REP. OF IRELAND, Lithuania, Iceland, Macedonia, Liechtenstein

A POTENTIALLY hazardous group for Mick McCarthy's Irish side, but one which they should be capable of coming through. It should be between them and Romania for top spot and much will depend on how each side does on those dodgy looking away trips.

MEN TO WATCH: Gheorghe Hagi (Romania), Mark Kennedy (Rep of Ireland)

GROUP SIX

Spain, Czech Republic, Slovakia, Yugoslavia, Malta, Faroe Islands

A FASCINATING group which pits the Czech Republic against Slovakia for the first time since Czechoslovakia split in two. There will be masses of national pride when they meet, but Spain will start as favourites and Yugoslavia can't be counted out, either.

MEN TO WATCH: Raul (Spain), Pavel Kuka (Czech Republic), Savo Milosevic (Yugoslavia)

GROUP NINE

Germany, Portugal, N. IRELAND, Ukraine, Albania, Armenia

IF NORTHERN IRELAND qualify for the finals it will be a sensational achievement. Germany and Portugal are two of the strongest sides in Europe at the moment and Bryan Hamilton's young side will have their work cut out against those two.

MEN TO WATCH: Jurgen Klinsmann (Germany), Rui Costa (Portugal), Gerard McMahon (N.Ireland)

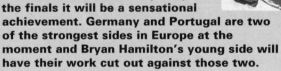

GROUP SEVEN

Holland, Belgium, Turkey, WALES, San Marino

YET AGAIN WALES find themselves in an extremely tough group. It seems to happen to them every time and they clearly face an uphill battle to come through in this sort of company. Their best hope is by winning their home games and picking up points wherever they can away, but Holland and Belgium look favourites

MEN TO WATCH: Edgar Davids (Holland), Phillipe Albert (Belgium), Ryan Giggs (Wales)

HOW IT WORKS

EUROPE WILL PROVIDE 15 finalists, but France qualify automatically as hosts. That leaves the 49 teams battling it out for 14 places.

The nine group winners will qualify by right, as will the team which finishes runners-up with the best record.

That will leave eight teams who will enter a play-off for the four remaining places.

There...easy, isn't it?!

Strange...

It's a weird and wonderful world out there...and football is about as weird and wonderful as it comes. And they don't come much stranger than this little lot...

DIEGO MARADONA made yet another comeback late last season, but this time in the boxing ring. The man with the 'Hand of God' swapped his boots for gloves to take part in a charity contest against former WBA flyweight champion Santos Laciar, one of Argentina's greatest ever fighters.

Judging by the look of him, dirty Diego would have been better off taking on a heavyweight. Perhaps it could be arranged for Mike Tyson to have a pop at him!

WE'VE HEARD OF die-hard fans but this is ridiculous...

A fan of Real Betis in Spain has taken things to new extremes by taking his father to every home game - even though he's dead!

The man's dying wish was to continue going to the matches, but his son ran into problems when he tried to take his ashes into the ground in a glass container.

That was ruled out as a security risk because the container was considered as a dangerous object, but the man's son knew how to get round the problem.

Now his late father enjoys the view at the Benito Villamarin Stadium...from the inside of a milk carton!

THERE WERE RED FACES all round in Verona last year, where authorities were forced to cancel plans to name a new stadium after Italy's 1938 World Cup winning goalkeeper Aldo Olivieri.

The idea was planned as a tribute to Olivieri but was scrapped when it was discovered he was still alive!

IT COULD ONLY HAPPEN in South America.

The Libertadores Cup is notorious for controversial incidents, but this year's tournament provided one of the most bizarre sendings-off of all time.

Espoli's Atualfo Valencia, in a match against Ecuador's other representative, Barcelona, was sent-off after being run over...by a golf cart!

The buggy hit him as it was being used to stretcher an injured player off the pitch, and Valencia was so incensed that he got up and punched the driver, leaving the ref no choice but to send him off.

SOUTH AFRICAN DEFENDER Mark Fish was one of the stars at last season's African Nations Cup, but some fans took their hero worship a little too far.

Many took dead fish to the games, some stuffed to the gills with South African flags, to wave in his honour. Still, it could have been worse...he could be called Mark Elephant!

.but true

THERE ARE PLENTY of superstitions in South American football, and one involved a black and white dog, named Biriba.

Little Biriba was adopted as a mascot by the Botafogo players back in 1948, and the club went on to win the Rio Championship that year.

Since then, Biriba's successors have been frequent visitors to the club and the latest is pictured here with star striker Tulio.

Wonder if Kevin Keegan's thought of trying it?

AND YOU THOUGHT the English FA was crazy...

An Italian amateur player was given a one-match ban last season...nine days after he was shot dead outside a bar in southern Italy!

Luigi Coluccio, 23, was killed while closing his bar in an incident which was thought to be connected with a mafia extortion racket.

He had been sent off the previous week while playing in the Calabrian amateur league and an official said the posthumous ban was unavoidable as the referee's report had been submitted before the shooting.

We gather, it's important in deciding who wins the Fair Play award.

Don't suppose Luigi really cares, though!

AND YOU THOUGHT the fans in this country wore some ridiculous outfits!

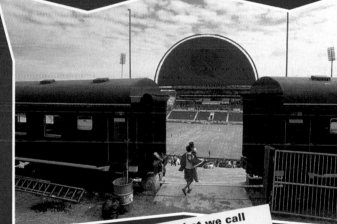

THERE WERE PROBABLY of few sighs of relief in the Seville dressing room when they were knocked out of last season's UFFA Cup by Barcelona.

Five of the players, led by pony-tailed defender Diego Rodriguez (left), had promised to shave off their hair if they reached the Quarter-Finals, a stage they had never managed before.

But Barcelona ended their hopes, and saved the Follicled Five a trip to the Barber of Seville.

NOW THESE are what we call executive boxes!

Believe it or not, that is what these train carriages were used for during the African Nations Cup in South Africa.

Still, at least they didn't have too far to go for the buffet car!

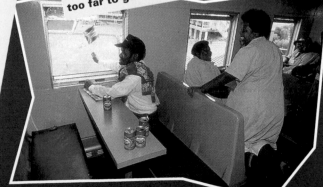

Iain **Dowie**

WEST HAM

GREAT SCOTS

THE TITLE RACE in Scotland last season was the closest it has been for years.

Celtic pushed Rangers all the way, before conceding defeat just two games from the end of a thrilling race.

It was a great battle and proved that Scottish football is on its way back to the standard it set during the mid 80s.

Then, there were four or five sides battling it out for the League Championship, but Rangers have been the dominant force for too long now.

And that is the challenge to the likes of Celtic, Aberdeen and Hearts - to break that all-conquering run.

Here, we examine the chances of that happening by looking at the strengths of those clubs, whilst paying tribute to The Gers...

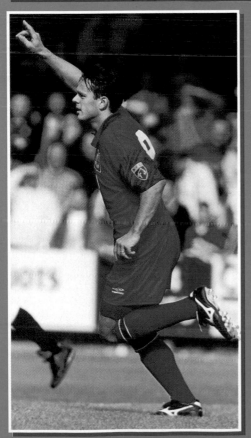

RANGERS made it eight League Championships in a row when they took the title last season.

In the closest finish for years, The Gers just held off the challenge off their great rivals Celtic to reclaim their crown.

And no-one can argue that they didn't deserve the title because they led the race virtually from start to finish.

And no-one did more to make it pieces of eight than Paul Gascoigne, the man the critics said was going to Glasgow for an easy life.

But Gazza proved that was not the case by claiming the first title medal of his career, and picking up the Player of the Year trophy.

Not a bad season's work for a player who was written off by many during the darkest days of his injury wrecked spell at Lazio.

But, in typical fashion, the lovable Geordie has bounced back with a vengeance.

He says: "My whole life is football and it's all gone so well for me here at Rangers. I've really enjoyed my first year and winning the title has to be the greatest day of my career.

"We had a brilliant party when we came back from Italia 90, and the other big day for me was when Spurs beat Arsenal in the 1991 FA Cup Semi-Final - but this tops the lot."

Rangers are the Premier prize guys

THE CRUNCHERS
The big games that won the title

September 30, 1995
Celtic 0 Rangers 2
The first League derby of the season and Rangers took a grip of the title race from there on in. Alex Cleland gave them the lead in the 44th minute and that man Gazza scored his first Old Firm goal midway through the second-half to clinch it. That win took them to the top of the table and they never looked back.

November 8, 1995
Kilmarnock 0 Rangers 2
Rangers were just three minutes from dropping two vital points in this one but they were rescued by two unlikely heroes. Centre-half Alan McLaren popped up to score the first goal in the 87th minute and mis-fit striker Oleg Salenko struck in the last minute to make sure of the points.

February 25, 1996
Aberdeen 0 Rangers 1
Trips to Pittodrie are never easy and, as the title nerves were beginning to show with Rangers

-eight!

PAUL GASCOIGNE: Gazza fully deserved his Player of the Year award. He totally won over the critics who said that he was going to Scotland for an easy life and that he should return to the Premiership. He proved them all wrong by turning in a string of committed, inspired performances. And 19 goals from midfield says it all about his contribution.

BRIAN LAUDRUP: Along with Gazza, probably the most gifted player in Scottish football. The great Dane has been superb in his two years in the Premier Division and his trickery and skills on the ball have wowed fans all over the country. His opponents are never quite so keen to see him, though!

ANDY GORAM: He's had his critics in recent years and even came close to quitting Ibrox after a bust-up with manager Walter Smith. But he knuckled down, won back his place in the side and has been impossible to shift ever since. Every good team is based on a solid defence and Rangers let in just 24 League goals last season. Nuff said!

and Celtic virtually neck and neck at the top, it was a game The Gers had to win. And they did with Gazza holding his nerve to convert a 32nd penalty.

March 30, 1996
Raith 2 Rangers 4
Rangers found themselves 2-1 down with just seven minutes to go and it looked as though they would make a fatal slip. But Ally McCoist came to the rescue. He'd already scored a first-half penalty, then he struck the equaliser in the 83rd and completed his hat-trick - to give Rangers the lead - a

minute from time. And there was still time for Gordon Durie to add a fourth in the 90th minute.

April 28, 1996
Rangers 3 Aberdeen 1
The day the title was won - and the day that Gazza won it. Rangers were given a shock when Brian Irvine gave The Dons a 19th minute lead, but from then on it was one-way traffic and a one-man show. Gazza equalised two minutes later, scored a wonder second with nine minutes to go and completed his first hat-trick for the club in the 86th minute.

Bhoys are back

And we're not going away says Burns

Celtic had their best season for years last term, but still ended it empty handed. They ran Rangers close for the title but eventually finished as runners-up and now they have to start all over again...

CELTIC finally started to climb out of Rangers' huge shadow last season, but they still couldn't quite make it into the limelight.

After years of misery and Ibrox domination, The Bhoys at last restored some pride and gave their fans something to shout about.

Unfortunately, they weren't quite able to give them the trophy they so desperately want.

They finished runners-up to Rangers in the League, and also saw their Scottish Cup hopes dashed at the Semi-Final stage by, yes...you've guessed it...Rangers!

But manager Tommy Burns refuses to be downhearted and promises his side's loyal supporters that the best is yet to come.

Burns has done a magnificent job since taking over from Lou Macari in 1995 and it seems certain that things will get better.

Certainly they will if he has his way. Burns insists: "We were disappointed to lose out in the title race, but I was very proud of my team.

"You must look at your own achievements to see how far you've progressed and we've come a hell of a long way in a year.

"My players couldn't have given any more last season and we will be stronger this year from having come so close.

"It's all about learning and if we can make the same progress again this year we can go far. We've set great standard for ourselves now and we won't be going away.

"The biggest achievement is that we've won back our supporters and now we know we have to take things a stage further."

Three-mendous

These are the men Burns will be hoping inspire Celtic to a title winning performance this season...

PIERRE VAN HOOYDONK

The big Dutchman took a little while to settle at Parkhead but he proved his worth last season. He felt that the side's style didn't suit him when Lou Macari was manager, but since Burns took over it has been goals all the way. He finished as the Premier Division's top scorer last term and a repeat performance could see Celtic finally get their hands on that Championship trophy.

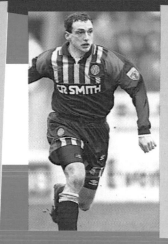

PAUL McSTAY

Mr Celtic, it seems as though he has been with the club for ever, but he is still as good as the day he started out. He is one of the most gifted midfield players Scotland has produced and his vision in the centre of the park creates so may openings for the front players. Now 32, he is running out of time to add another Championship medal to his collection.

TOSH McKINLAY

A fairly late bloomer, but he is now playing at the top of his form. Last season was his first for Celtic after lengthy spells at both Dundee and Hearts, but it was a memorable one for him as he was capped by Scotland for the first time. Now he will be looking to continue that form and inspire The Bhoys to glory.

Gaz-tastic

TOMMY BURNS is in no doubt what was the difference between Celtic and Rangers last season - Paul Gascoigne.

Gazza was crowned Player of the Year in his first season in the Premier Division, and Burns reckons he fully deserved the accolade.

The Celtic boss says: "Gascoigne basically won the League for Rangers. He's been a quite sensational signing.

"There's not a team in the world who would not want someone like that in their side. The goals he got in the game against Aberdeen which clinched the title for them were out of this world - but then only Gazza can score goals like that.

"He is one of the best players in the world."

The New

Rangers and Celtic once again dominated Scottish football last season and the gauntlet has been thrown down for the others to close the gap. Aberdeen and Hearts look the most likely challengers...

THREE YEARS AGO, Hearts avoided relegation by just two points.

Two years ago, Aberdeen needed a play-off win over Dunfermline to avoid the drop.

Last season, The Dons finished third. The men from Tynecastle were one place behind them.

That is the measure of their improvement and both demonstrated that by reaching domestic Cup Finals last term - Aberdeen in the Cola-Cola Cup and Hearts in the Scottish Cup.

Both have proved they can take on the Glasgow giants of Rangers and Celtic in one-off games, but the real test is whether they can sustain it over the season.

That is the challenge to them now as they attempt to gatecrash the title race, which was played out solely between the Old Firm last term.

For the sake of Scottish football it needs another team to mount a serious challenge to the big two, and both of these sides now look capable of doing that.

Both have a wealth of young talent at their disposal, and they are hungry for success.

And none more so than Hearts striker Allan Johnston.

He insists: "We're more confident now and the side has got amazing self-belief. We don't ever go into a match thinking anyone is better than us.

"The manager, Jim Jeffries, has given us that belief and we're really enjoying life now.

"Hearts is the biggest club outside the Old Firm and a lot of people outside Scotland don't realise that."

Now the test for Hearts, and Aberdeen, is to prove they are big enough to mix it with the big boys. These are just a few of the guys who will be out to do just that in the coming seasons...

THE HEARTS HEROES

GARY LOCKE
The captain of the side at just 21, he is Hearts through and through. When he is not playing, he travels to the games with his mates and stands with them on the terraces rather than sitting in the directors' box. An Under-21 international, he seems certain to go and play for the senior side

ALAN JOHNSTON
Nicknamed 'Magic' and widely regarded as one of the most naturally gifted players ever to come out of Scotland. A winger with bags of tricks and skill, he terrorises opposition defenders when he is in the mood and is virtually impossible to stop.

Firm

But can they end the Glasgow grip?

THE DONS DIAMONDS

SCOTT BOOTH

One of Scotland's rising stars, he is already a vital member of the international side at just 24. He has been at Aberdeen all his career and, after Eoin Jess' transfer to Coventry, he has emerged as Pittodrie's main man.

STEPHEN GLASS

Talented midfielder who only turned 20 in the summer, but has already proved his ability with the Scottish Under-21 side. He has tremendous ability coupled with an eye for goal, as he proved by finishing as the club's top scorer last season.

PAUL RITCHIE

Most Hearts fans reckon he is the new Alan McLaren - they are just hoping they can keep hold of him a bit longer than his famous predecessor. A former captain of the Scotland Under-18 side, he is strong and quick and has a brilliant left foot.

ALAN McMANUS

Given a free transfer under former boss Tommy McLean, but was handed another chance by Jeffries last season and hasn't looked back since. A cultured defender, he forms an excellent partnership with Ritchie.

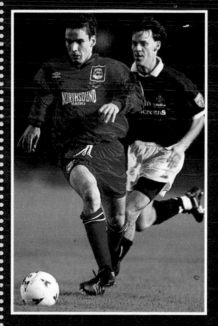

JAMIE BUCHAN

If he proves to be half the player his father was then he will be a huge star. Buchan junior is the son of former Dons favourite, Martin, and he has set about emulating his famous dad in the best possible way with a string of excellent performances in the centre of defence. Has a big future in the game.

DEAN WINDASS

Proved to be a big hit last season following his £750,000 move from Hull and even greater things will be expected of him in the future. He proved his goalscoring ability with Hull and followed on from there last term, and if he can bag a few more this season who knows what Aberdeen could achieve.

Just Champion

Rangers may have cacried off the biggest trophy of all in Scotland, but there were three other sides celebrating Championship-winning seasons. SHOOT pays tribute to those sides...

First Division Champions DUNFERMLINE

A year after just missing out on a place in the Premier Division, Dunfermline were crowned First Division Champions and regained their place among the big boys.

Twelve months earlier they had fallen at the final hurdle when they crashed in a play-off decider with Aberdeen, but last season they made no mistakes.

They were there or thereabouts among the leading pack all season and finally ran out comfortable winners, finishing four points clear of second placed Dundee United.

But now they've reached the holy grail of the top flight the test is to make sure they stay there.

The hard work has only just begun.

Second Division Champions STIRLING ALBION

Like Dunfermline, they made amends for the disappointment of the previous season.

On that occasion they found themselves edged out of the promotion frame, missing out on the second promotion spot by just two points from Dumbarton.

But the fate of the team which pipped them last year wil serve as Albion's greatest motivation this year.

Stirling ran away with the Second Division title, finishing a massive 14 points clear of East Fife, but like Dunfermline, the hard work is still to be done.

Dumbarton found that out to their cost as they finished rock bottom of the First Division, collecting just three wins, 11 points and ending up 25 points adrift of second from bottom Hamilton.

Stirling, you have been warned.

Third Division Champions LIVINGSTON

This must have been one of the turnarounds of all time.

A year ago, Meadowbank were relegated from the Second Division and the future looked bleak.

Then came a change of name - to Livingston - a change of ground, and a massive change in fortune.

A new stadium was built, a new team was born, and they celebrated in superb style by taking the Third Division title.

Meadowbank may have gone, but the best days could still be to come.

FAB
FOREIGNERS

What a season it was for the Premiership with a fabulous array of foreign players coming to England's shores to show off their soccer skills in the best league in the world.

The likes of Ruud Gullit, David Ginola, Georgiou Kinkladze, Dennis Bergkamp, and of course, the Football Writers' Footballer of the Year - Eric Cantona - thrilled packed crowds throughout the land.

Scotland too, had its fair share of foreign superstars with Pierre Van Hooeydonk and Erik Bo Anderson just two of the players to light up the game North of the Border.

SHOOT has picked seven foreign stars who graced the top flight last season and brings you an insight into just what makes them tick...

Eric Cantona

From being a target of abuse, Eric Cantona has become a figure of respect – the Football Writers' unanimous choice as Footballer of the Year.

Back in France they greeted the news with a characteristic Gallic shrug, a few 'Sacra Bleu's and an occasional 'Mon Dieu'.

Could this be the same Eric Cantona who called their national team's coach a bag of something or other, the same Eric Cantona who had punch-ups with both the opposition and his team-mates, and the same Eric Cantona who walked out on French football for good after one brush too many with the authorities? Mais oui!

For our French readers - 'ere are a few of the most interesting things about Eric...

- As a kid he used to kick a ball about outside his dad's workplace while his dad was inside painting.
- He comes from the Callols region of France. The people there consider themselves only partly French, they mostly think of themselves as independent, although Eric insists that he is French at heart.
- He enjoys class French cuisine and has several favourite French restaurants in the North of England.
- He likes music and can play the violin better than average.
- He has now won four Championships out of a possible five since he came to England.
- He has had a book of poems published and is also well into painting and sculpture. He has also done some catwalk modelling.

STEVE BRUCE ON BERGKAMP

"Eric is on a totally different level to everyone else. He is a brilliant player. He has been phenomenal this season, both in matches and in his work in training."

"It is a marvellous club and I have come to love it very much. The supporters are wonderful and have helped me a lot. Also the manager and the players are all very special. That is why I have no interest in joining any other club."

ERIC CANTONA

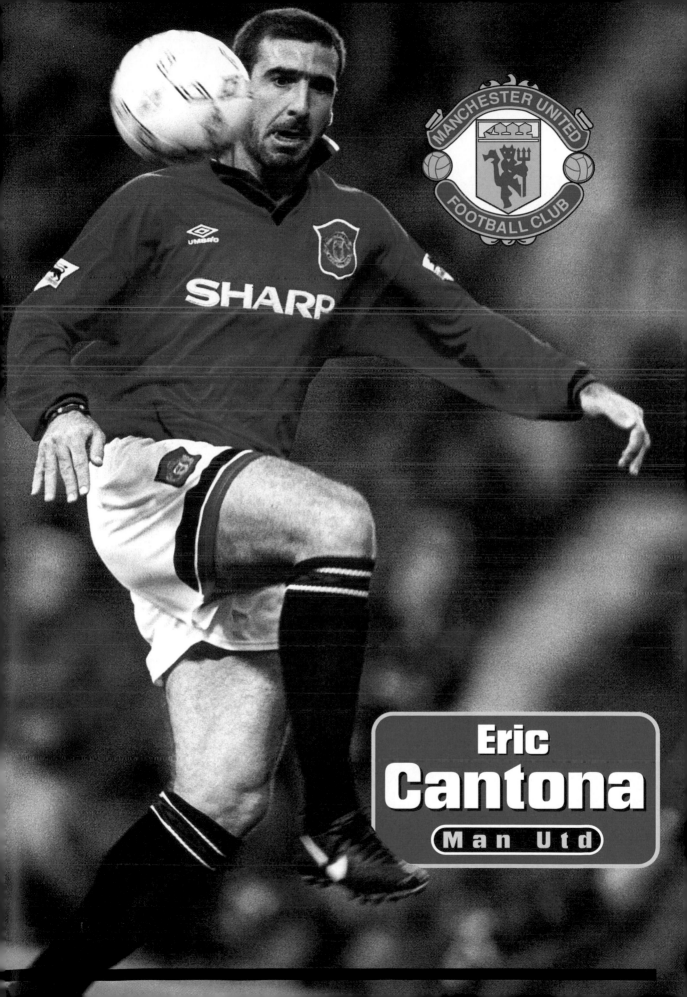

Ruud Gullit

The fans can't stop singing the Blues since they were tangoed by Dutch international legend Ruud Gullit.

Just when it seemed his playing career was coming to an end, he moved to London and became the toast of the town.

His inspirational performances for Chelsea helped them to the FA Cup Semi-Finals and some classic Premiership displays and down at The Bridge, they will be hoping he decides to stay with Chelsea - for a very, very long time.

Here are some super facts about Holland's greatest export to Chelsea...

● He is passionately interested in politics and when he finally decides to move out of football, don't be surprised to see him campaign for voters.

● His father was an international for Surinam but Ruud's dream was to play for Holland.

● It is true that he loves reggae and has had hit records with his own band on the continent, but he also likes many other types of music.

● He made his senior playing debut when he was only 16. He was still a teenager when he was offered to Arsenal and they turned him down.

● He keeps his rasta hairstyle simply because he likes it that way - it's not an expression of his religion.

● He can speak four laguages fluently - Dutch, English, German and Italian.

DENNIS WISE ON GULLIT
"You can see why he is considered world class. He is a terrific player. He has done it all and virtually won it all.
His style and quality of play has fitted in very well at Chelsea and given us a lot of extra options."

"I have felt more relaxed since I have been at Chelsea than I have for a long time. That is because I am enjoying playing good football. I have enjoyed every minute of it and I believe the potential here is tremendous."

RUUD GULLIT

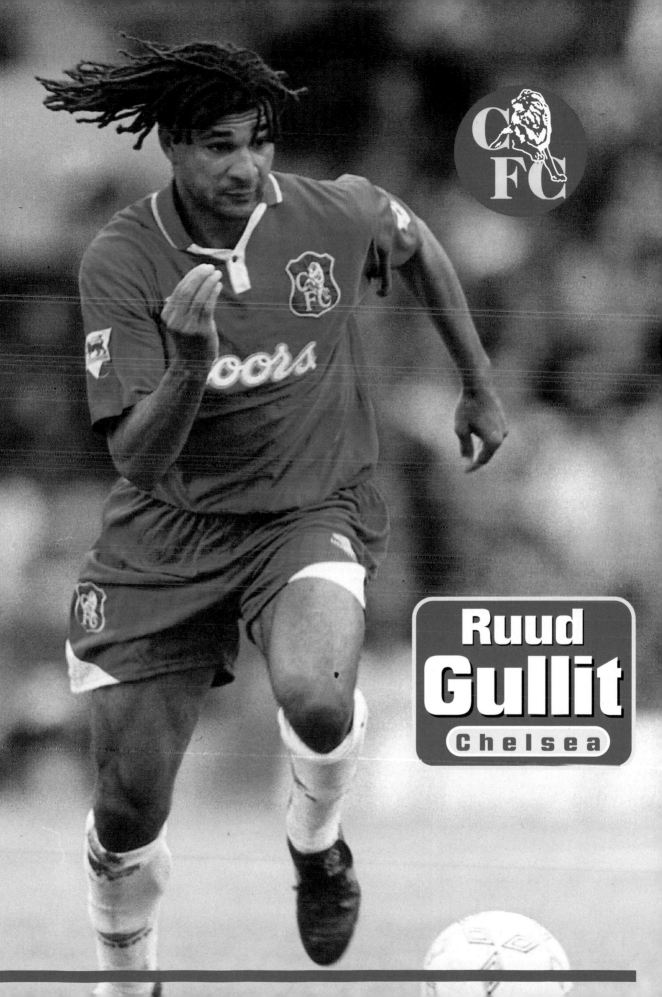

Ruud **Gullit**
Chelsea

David Ginola

They seek him here and they seek him there, defenders seek Ginola everywhere.

With more twists and turns than the French revolution, David Ginola has caused havoc among Premiership defences since he signed for Newcastle in the summer of 1995.

He has also become the darling of female fans up and down Britain, even those who don't like Newcastle. Strangely, there are many who find him more appealing than Peter Beardsley! Funny thing the female mind!

Still, Beardo doesn't care just so long as Ginola does his bit in getting the ball into the net.

And if you thought you knew all there was to know about him, take a quick look at this little lot...

● He was born in trendy St. Tropez, the haunt of millionaires and models in the South of France.
● He is something of a music expert with more than 700 CDs.
● He is instantly recognised if he tries to go shopping in Newcastle and is usually mobbed.
● He likes Italian food, Italian wine and Italian restaurants. Guess where he would like to play one day?
● He has said that when he retires from playing he would like to do something completely different, like take his family back-packing up the Amazon. Lucky family!
● If you want an autograph, be polite. He rarely refuses but likes good manners.

KEVIN KEEGAN ON GINOLA
"I knew he could do a good job for us and he has. He has become a huge favourite with the fans and well liked and respected by his team-mates. He enjoys being here and a medal or two will put the icing on the cake."

"I am very happy here. The club is huge with enormous support. I have been delighted with playing for Newcastle. I came because of Kevin Keegan and players like Peter Beardsley, Les Ferdinand and Philippe Albert. I have not been disappointed."

DAVID GINOLA

David
Ginola
Newcastle

Dennis Bergkamp

ARSENAL

Dennis Bergkamp

Ask any Arsenal player and they will tell you that Dennis Bergkamp is worth every penny of the club record £7.5 million that it took to buy him from Inter.

Dennis took a few weeks to settle when he first arrived but then the Flying Dutchman began to get his clogs sorted out and by the end of last season his displays were as good as any in the Premier.

His last goal of the season was breathtaking and had Bolton goalkeeper Keith Branagan spinning like a windmill. Dennis was delighted his goal guaranteed a place in the UEFA Cup for The Gunners. After all, they might come face to face with his old pals in Italy.

We all know that Dennis was a big Spurs fan but did you know these big facts...

● From October 1988 to January 1989 he scored in ten consecutive League matches for Ajax, a Dutch league record.

● At the age of 18 he appeared in the ECWC Final of 1987 and won it with Ajax.

● He enjoys golf and loves snooker and would really like to have become a world snooker champion like Stephen Hendry.

● He has three brothers and they all play senior amateur football in Holland.

● He met his wife while they were holidaying with their respective families and were staying on the same camp site.

● He was Footballer of the Year in Holland in 1992 and dearly wants to earn the same honour here.

TONY ADAMS ON BERGKAMP

"The fans think the world of him. He is a great player - a terrific passer with great skills who can lose a defender with just one movement, and he has proved that he can score goals as well. World class."

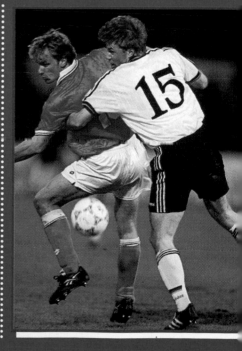

"I always wanted to play in England and, while it is a little ironic playing for the team who are rivals to the one who were my favourites, I have been having a great time. The Arsenal supporters are excellent. They are noisy, back you all the way and really know their football."

DENNIS BERGKAMP

Tony Yeboah

Golden goals for Ghana, golden goals in Germany and sensational scoring for Leeds. That's a normal day's work for Tony Yeboah and gave Elland Road fans their few thrilling moments of last season. Now he is leading the charge again in the hunt for goals that can put Leeds back on the map of supersides. He is a class act and manager Howard Wilkinson's chief problem was not how to motivate him, but how to find someone good enough to play alongside him. Here are a few Yeboah extras for your file...

● He began playing soccer in the streets of Kusami in Ghana, often barefooted.
● He has been Leeds' top scorer for two seasons.
● He once had a serious leg injury which baffled specialists. It was cured by ointment from an

GARY MCALLISTER ON YEBOAH
"He is one of the most lethal finishers I have ever seen. He is big, strong and skilful, and sheer class. He breaks goalkeeper's hearts.

African witchdoctor!
● He has three brothers, five sisters, a wife and two daughters.. and a long birthday list.
● Part of his Leeds sponsorship was by a Yorkshire pudding company.
● He is a snappy dresser and generally said to be a nice bloke. And he has this to say...

"I want to win things with Leeds. When I came here on loan everyone was really good to me and the fans were marvellous. I knew I wanted to stay longer than just a few months. I believe there are better days ahead for Leeds."

TONY YEBOAH

Tony **Yeboah**
Leeds

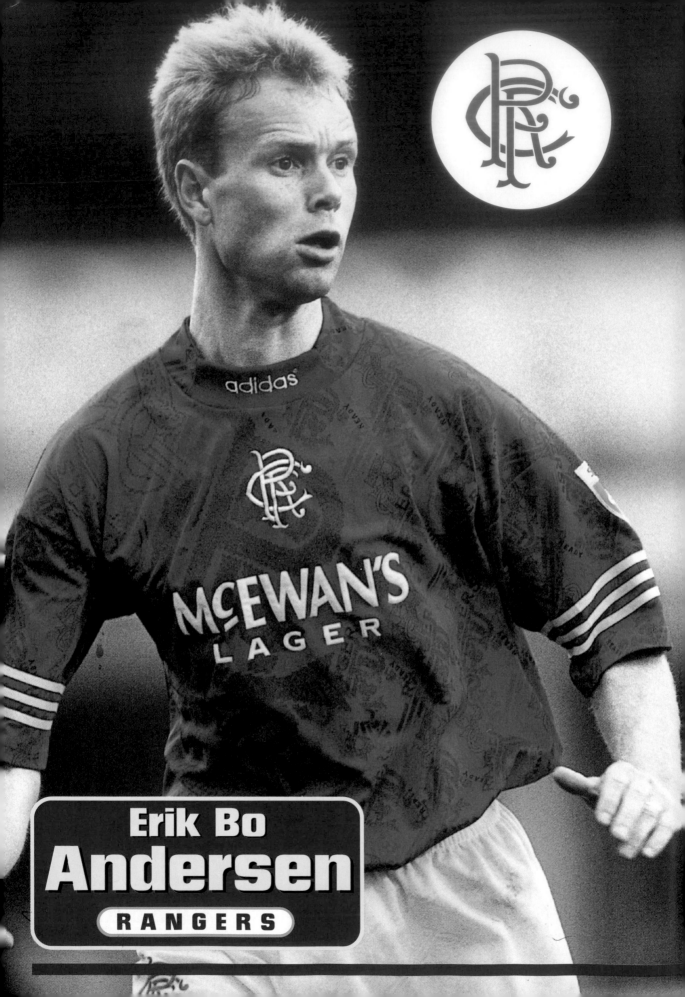

Erik Bo Andersen

RANGERS

Erik Bo Andersen

Within two months of Erik Bo Andersen's arrival in British football his club had won the Scottish Premier League title. Not bad eh? Of course, Rangers were probably going to win the title for an eighth successive season anyway but if you are going to jump ship, better to land on a speedboat than a tug as Eric Cantona might say.

The Danish international signed up with Rangers at just the right time and now wants to link up with his fellow ex-pat Danes to plot his country's assault on the World Cup - after all there are enough great Danes in Britain to form their own team.

If you thought you knew all about Bo, think again, like this for instance...

● His last matches before he joined Rangers in March were in Thailand where he was on tour with Denmark.
● Rangers snatched him from under the noses of Inter, Everton, Man City, Southampton and, more importantly, Celtic, who had put in a bid of £1.25 million.
● He didn't start playing seriously until he was 20 because he wanted to graduate at university first.
● There was a slight hitch before he signed because he was worried about his spaniel dog going into quarantine. But kennels were found nearby.
● In his last full season with Aalborg, he scored 24 goals in 32 League matches including three hat-tricks. It was the League's highest individual tally for 14 years.
● His international debut for Denmark was in April, 1995 when he came on as a second-half sub and helped them win 1-0 over Macedonia.
So what made him join Rangers?

WALTER SMITH ON ERIK BO ANDERSEN

"He is an excellent player who already has a great pedigree in the game. He is a proven scorer and international player, with a record that speaks for itself. He has settled in well and I believe that the 1996-97 season will see him at his very best."

"Rangers are one of the top clubs in Europe and everyone knows that. I knew when they came in for me I had to sign for them. Then I phoned Brian Laudrup and the fact that he was already at Ibrox and spoke glowingly of the club finally made my mind up." -

ERIK BO ANDERSEN

Georgi Kinkladze

So Manchester City went down last season but will they stay down? Not likely - not if Georgiou Kinkladze has anything to do with it.

They've nicknamed him Kinky but it could be Jinky because he leaves opponents totally in a daze as he jinks his way between them on his path to goal.

It was one of those 'if only' seasons for City last time but the little Georgian international holds the Maine Road key to a quick return. He unlocks tight defences and latches on to chances. He'll get City out of their First Division jail.

But what of Georgiou's other secrets? Did you know...

● His mum wanted him to take up folk dancing rather than soccer!
● He looks upon himself as an ambassador for his country and works hard to impress.
● To help him build himself up, he was treated to Chinese meals and Tango.
● He had terrible language problems when he first arrived but now speaks English like a....Mancunian.
● He is left footed and believes he is useless with his right. He's wrong.
● He likes Oasis and Georgian folk music.
    And he loves Manchester...

ALAN BALL ON KINKY

"In today's market we got him cheap. The fans adore him and so does everyone at the club. I said from day one that this kid would have you up on the rafters and he has."

"I was thrilled when I knew I was coming to play in English football and I have not been disappointed. It was a pity we were relegated but I think sometimes that when things go wrong it gives you more strength. Manchester is a wonderful city and everyone has been very kind. It is home."

GEORGI KINKLADZE

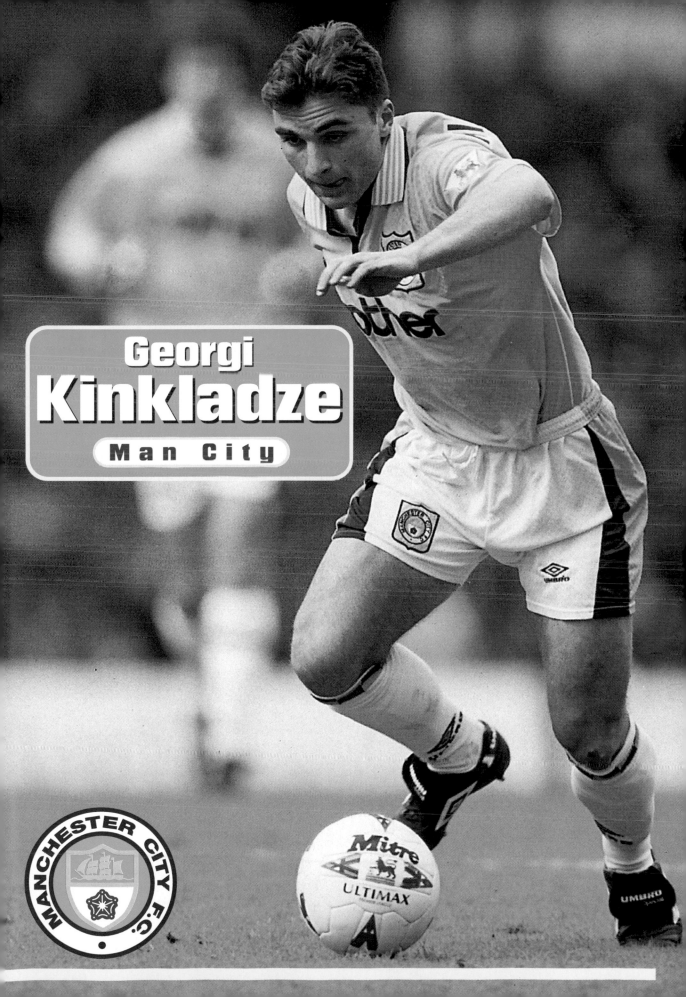

Georgi **Kinkladze**

Man City

FOREIGN LEGION

Here's your club-by-club guide to the foreign stars who have 'satellite' our heavenly soccer in 1996...

ARSENAL
Dennis Bergkamp *(Holland)*
Glenn Helder *(Holland)*
John Jensen *(Denmark)*

ASTON VILLA
Mark Bosnich *(Australia)*
Savo Milosevic *(Yugoslavia)*
Dwight Yorke *(Trinidad and Tobago)*

BLACKBURN
Henning Berg *(Norway)*
Lars Bohinen *(Norway)*

CHELSEA
Dmitri Kharine *(Russia)*
Ruud Gullit *(Holland)*
Jakob Kjeldberg *(Denmark)*
Erland Johnsen *(Norway)*
Dan Petrescu *(Romania)*

COVENTRY
Carlos Batista *(Portugal)*
Isaias Marques Soares *(Portugal)*
Nii Lamptey *(Ghana)*
Peter Ndlovu *(Zimbabwe)*

DERBY
Igor Stimac *(Croatia)*

EVERTON
Andrei Kanchelskis *(Russia)*
Anders Limpar *(Sweden)*
Daniel Amokachi *(Nigeria)*
Marc Hottiger *(Switzerland)*

LEEDS
Lucas Radebe *(South Africa)*
Philomen Masinga *(South Africa)*
Tony Yeboah *(Ghana)*
Tomas Brolin *(Sweden)*

LIVERPOOL
Stig Inge Bjornebye *(Norway)*

MANCHESTER UNITED
Peter Schmeichel *(Denmark)*
Eric Cantona *(France)*

MIDDLESBROUGH
Jaime Moreno *(Bolivia)*
Jan-Aage Fjortoft *(Norway)*
Branco *(Brazil)*
Juninho *(Brazil)*

NEWCASTLE
Pavel Srnicek *(Czechoslovakia)*
Philippe Albert *(Belgium)*
David Ginola *(France)*
Faustino Asprilla *(Colombia)*

NOTTINGHAM FOREST
Alf Inge Haaland *(Norway)*
Bryan Roy *(Holland)*
Andrea Silenzi *(Italy)*

SHEFFIELD WEDNESDAY
Klas Ingesson *(Sweden)*
Darko Kovacevic *(Yugoslavia)*
Dejan Stefanovic *(Yugoslovia)*
Regi Blinker *(Holland)*
Marc Degryse *(Belgium)*

SOUTHAMPTON
Ken Monkou *(Holland)*

SUNDERLAND
Darisz Kubicki *(Poland)*

TOTTENHAM
Erik Thorstvedt *(Norway)*

WEST HAM
Ludek Miklosko *(Czech Republic)*
Marc Rieper *Denmark)*

Robbie Slater *(Australia)*
Dani *(Portugal)*
Jerome Boere *(Holland)*
Slaven Bilic *(Croatia)*

WIMBLEDON
Efan Ekoku *(Nigeria)*
Oyvind Leonhardsen *(Norway)*

CELTIC
Pierre Van Hooydonk *(Holland)*
Andreas Thom *(Germany)*
Jorge Cadete *(Portugal)*
Morten Wieghorst *(Denmark)*

HEARTS
Gilles Rousset *(France)*
Dragole Lekovic *(Croatia)*

MOTHERWELL
Mitchel Van Der Gaag *(Holland)*

RAITH ROVERS
Anthony Rougier *(Trinidad and Tobago)*
Miodrag Krivokapic *(Croatia)*

RANGERS
Brian Laudrup *(Denmark)*
Erik Bo Andersen *(Denmark)*
Peter Van Vossen *(Holland)*
Gordan Petric *(Croatia)*
Theo Snelders *(Holland)*

IT'S A FUNNY OLD GAME!

Stars in their Eyes

Around the World in 80 seconds!

Amazing... but true!

WORLD

SHOOT goes globe trotting with the stars

GRAHAM TAYLOR (New York)
Oh no, he's back in the running for the England job!

WARREN BARTON (London)
'Can I get down off this ladder now?'

TREVOR STEVEN (Marseille)
Don't that look boat-iful, eh?

TIM FLOWERS (Washington)
'He might be President, but can he balance a ball like this?'

JUNINHO (Sao Paulo)
'Come on then, see if you can get it off me'

ALAN SHEARER (Venice)
You'd better duck, or it will be Shear agony

PARTY

These players, what are they like? They can't go anywhere without their favourite footy mag. Whenever they're off on their travels, we have to go to, too. Oh well, dirty job...

SCOTT GEMMILL (Faroe Islands)
'Do a pic for SHOOT, they said. Go somewhere sunny, they said. Doh!'

RYAN GIGGS (Moscow)
'If you'd like to step this way for the sightseeing tour ladies'

NIGEL CLOUGH (Sydney)
'Oh yes, we love a bit of opera, don't we Sydney?'

PETER SCHMEICHEL (Istanbul)
'Yeah, it's not bad, but how will you get the net on it?'

GARY LINEKER (Milan)
Gary models the latest bit of Italian designer wear

BOBBY ROBSON (Egypt)
Bobby poses with his favourite player - Nigel Sphinx!

STARS IN THEIR EYES

Yeah, and in their eyes only by the look of it!

Come on, admit it, we all reckon we're gonna play for England don't we? And we're not the only ones. Even stars of stage and screen seem convinced they are set to take the footy world by storm. Do you think we oughta tell 'em?

Look at the athleticism, the agility, the grim face of determination, it could only be...a DJ pretending to be a goalkeeper! Sorry, Chrissie babe, we love your show, but you should leave this to the pros.

It's always been Sean Bean's ambition to play at Bramall Lane, the home of his beloved Sheffield United. He finally got his wish in the film When Saturday Comes, and he even got to score a goal!

Did you know that comedian Bradley Walsh used to actually be a pro footballer? Apparently though, before he could really make his mark, he had to limp out of the game with a knee injury. Wonder which knee?

Our Curly, also known as actor Kevin Kennedy, is a big Man City fan and loves cheering the boys on. Mind you, the way they've been getting on lately, maybe he should take his boots with him to Maine Road!

Have I got moves for you? Angus Deayton battles it out with London's Burning star Glen Murphy. As he used to be a boxing champ, our money's on the man with the hose.

Not a bad style by the boy Damon, but we don't reckon Alan Shearer has got too much to worry about, just yet. But perhaps it's not too late. After all, he is a Chelsea fan and you know what they say...Blur is the Colour!

American Ruby Wax might not quite have grasped all there is to know about our great game but, like all top players, she's well up for a cuddle after scoring. David Seaman is the lucky chappie!

Ooh, no wonder they scrapped the Shane Ritchie Experience if this is the sort of thing he gets up to. Right dodgy challenge. Mind you, it is only Stan Boardroom so that's fair enough then!

BEST OF In the NET

LOG ON
LOG ON
LOG ON
LOG ON
LOG ON
LOG ON
LOG ON
LOG ON
LOG ON
LOG ON

DON'T PICK UP THE "BACKPASS"!

THE ULTIMATE CHALLENGE FOR THE MODERN 'KEEPER

STILL VERY POOR!

This time with DAVID JAMES

We've carefully placed a pair of well-known and well-loved words at David's feet. If he picks up the one that means "orange root crop vegetable" then he'll move on to future greatness with Liverpool, and, possibly, England, but if he picks up the other then it's all BAD, BAD, BAD!!!

And, oh, yes, we've blind-folded him!

So let's see how he got on then... OH DEAR!

"CARROT" "BACKPASS"

It's the first good result Harry's had in a cup for ages!

The Net reveals who's tested positive for rugs...

The Golden Syrup Awards

And this year's winner is John Aldridge – no wonder he likes it in Tranmere where everyone *looks* like this!

THE BEAUTIFUL GAME

Here DAVID GINOLA shows you how to make your fly-away hair problems a thing of the past

Is There FOOTBALL on Other Planets?
This week: NEPTUNE

IT IS VERY cold and bleak on the surface of Neptune and therefore football is mostly played under-ground in centrally-heated warrens. Goals, however, can only be scored 'topside' and are all scored with the head as the Nepts have no feet.

Can I have my ball back?

OH DEAR, Brian was enjoying a nice little (!) kick-around in his back garden with a few of the lads from the Villa squad, but ever since Dwight Yorke headed the ball into his next door neighbour's garden two hours ago he's been in turmoil. Mrs Tyger has gone wild, you see, and not even the crack team of negotiators he's brought in can break the deadlock.

What's on T.V.?

Moonlighting

Apparently Vinnie's still putting in a few hours as a HOD CARRIER

Father Ted

Shin Pads

Helpful notes the stars tuck down their socks

WITH
Jason McAteer

Left

Right

Dead Ball Specialists

EXCLUSIVE! SHOOT brings you the true stories of men who cannot live with their soccer shame!

This top Italian star who wishes only to be known as Roberto would only agree to an interview on the understanding he did not have to face our cameras…

BAGGIO 19

ROBERTO: Si, it still causes me much pain to tell my tale, but I remember it like it was only yesterday. I am running like a young Duke of Milan towards the ball and I striko it with as much power as a free kick from forty of your yards it deserve.

When the ball it leave the stadium I know that I have caught it in the special way to bend it around the entire of Naples. So I wait and the crowd wait, and the opposition, how you say, 'goalie' he is much restless. And then – Ka-Booma! – the ball it reappear and slam against the underside of the crossbar with a tremendous power. As it hit the back of the net the crowd they go wild and everyone agree it is making a very, very fine goal!

Sadly the ball it never recover and it die alone and unloved in the back of a cupboard. And I am so sorry, so very, very sorry…

THE ROAD TO WEMBLEY

The M62

with LIVERPOOL'S ROBBIE FOWLER

"OBVIOUSLY, AS I'M still only twelve I'm not allowed to drive, but if I was I know just the road to get me out of Bootle and off in the direction of the Twin Towers. And that's the M62, wack. It's a right sound and bangin' stretch of tarmac. And you can bet your bib that me, Redders, Macca and Babbsy get down there as often as possible to watch the traffic nipping past on a Saturday before going home for an early night.

Luckily, Roy Evans our coach driver is as fond of the old '62 as we are, so maybe we'll be off down it again soon".

OASIS' NOEL IS NEW ENGLAND BOSS!

Gallagher's Grafters

1. Eike Immel **Man City**
2. Ian Brightwell **Man City**
3. Francis Lee **Man City**
4. Steve Lomas **Man City**
5. Keith Curle **Man City**
6. Kit Symons **Man City**
7. Georgi Kinkladze **Man City**
8. Colin Bell **Man City**
9. Michael Brown **Man City**
10. Nick Summerbee **Man City**
11. Nigel Clough **Man City**
SUBS

Dennis Tueart **Man City**
Rodney Marsh **Man City**

the small world of BABY GAZZA

What? That's me in fifteen years time? WAAAAAAAAAHHHH!

IT'S CRAZY BUT TRUE!?

IT'S CRAZY, SPACE-WASTING BUT TRUE!?

"Right then youse lot, SHUT UP! and LISTEN UP!

Now that I'm gaffer we'll start doing things MY WAY! So from now on we'll be playing a style that favours all out ATTACK! And while we're ATTACKING! we'll all be doing a fair bit of SHOUTING, SWEARING and FIGHTING 'n' stuff. Which is SOUND!

Oh yeah, Our Kid's gonna be helpin' out by coaching the team to develop their

REFUELLING PROBLEMS! And sewing OASIS! logos onto the front of the shirts too. Which is also SOUND!

And we're all be wearing black arm-bands for JOHN LENNON !and trainers instead of footy boots 'cos they're way COOLER!

Oh yeah, AND! I've got a song about it! SOUND!"

QUIT
QUIT
QUIT
QUIT
QUIT
QUIT
QUIT
QUIT

QUIT

WOW!
That's absolutely amazing

They say that football is a funny old game and judging by some of these astonishing stats and facts, it certainly is...

Even as a ten-year-old Ian Rush looked destined to become a top goalscorer. As a schoolboy at St Mary's Primary School he once scored all eight goals in an 8-4 win. The following week, he got the lot in a 6-4 victory against the same side!

Someone must have been blind the day a young Alan Shearer turned up for a trial at Newcastle. Why? Because they played him in GOAL, that's why!

Paul Gascoigne must hate playing on New Year's Day. In 1989, he missed Newcastle's game through injury, in 1990 he cracked his left arm and was out for a month, and in 1991 he was sent-off. Oh well, Happy New Year!

While he was doing his National Service, former Man United great Bobby Charlton won the high jump, javelin and 880 yards race at an Army sports day.

In December 1990, Wolves goalkeeper Mike Stowell hired a tractor to beat the snow storms in the West Midlands in

The day after Trevor Francis signed for Forest to become the country's first £1m player he played for the A team in a game at Notts County.

order to report for his first international duty with the England B team.

On January 10, 1989 Watford scored with their first touch of the ball in an FA Cup Third Round replay at home to Newcastle. Newcastle kicked off and kept possession until goalkeeper Dave Beasant was penalised for carrying the ball outside the penalty area. From Watford's free-kick, Neil Redfearn scored.

Ian St John once scored a hat-trick in just two-and-a-half minutes playing for Motherwell at Hibernian in a Scottish

Rangers 'keeper Andy Goram used to play cricket for Scotland, but he was banned by the Ibrox club in case he got injured.

Matt Le Tissier wasn't the first Jersey born player to star in the Football League. Oh no. The first Channel Islander to turn pro was Eric Hurel, who joined Everton from St Helier in April 1936.

League Cup tie. Motherwell won 3-1.

Everton were the first club in Britain to introduce a stripe down the seams of their shorts.

When England beat Malta 5-0 at Wembley in May 1971, goalkeeper Gordon Banks touched the ball only four times, all from back-passes.

In January 1991, St Albans City donated their entire first team kit to the

Kuwaiti national team.

In January 1975, Bobby Gould, now boss of Wales, was taken off at half-time of West Ham's 2-1 FA Cup Third Round win against Southampton when it was discovered he had broken a leg after just 15 minutes! And he still managed to score one of West Ham's goals!

in November 1983, during an injury crisis at Watford, the club placed this advert in The Times: Wanted:

Professional footballers, men (or women) aged 18-80, preference given to applicants with two arms and two legs in working order.

Blackburn's Colin Hendry once fell foul of the law during a match. He went to retrieve the ball when it went out of play and, as it had rolled towards a policewoman, he thought it would be fun to knock her hat over her eyes. But, it completely flew off her head and he received a stern warning!

Although Pele never played at Wembley, he did make one appearances in London. In March 1973, he played for Brazilian side Santos against Fulham at Craven Cottage. Fulham won 2-1.

In April 1982, during the Falklands War, Stockport considered changing their colours because they matched the Argentine national kit.

Vinnie Jones is in the record books for the fastest ever booking. In a game for Sheffield United against Man City in January 1991, he got a yellow card for fouling Peter Reid after just FIVE SECONDS! After 55 minutes, he was sent-off for another foul on Reid.

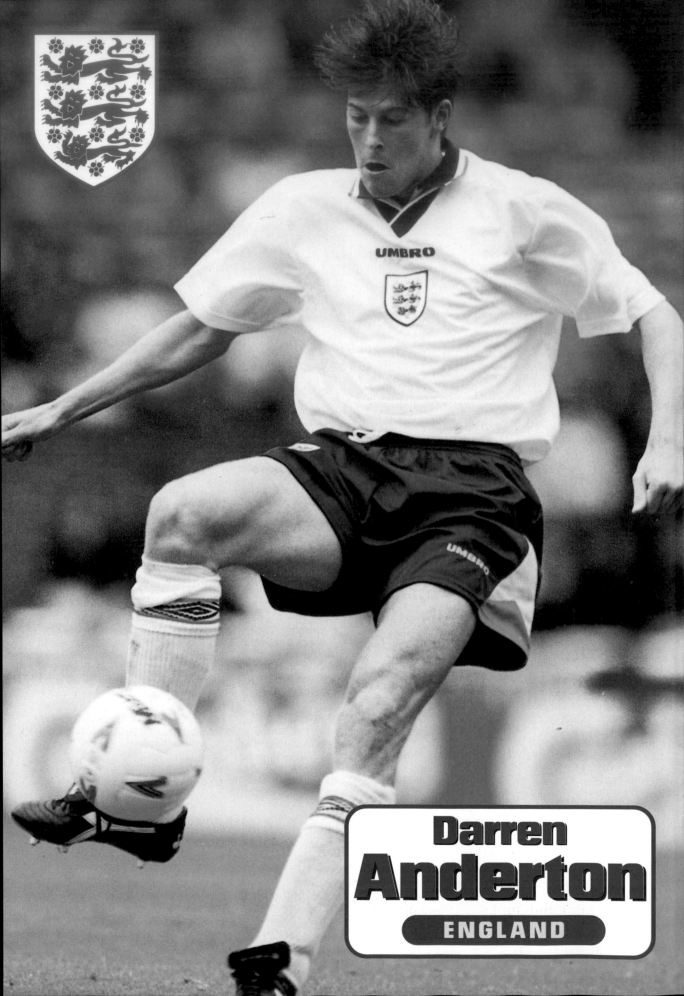

Darren Anderton

ENGLAND

CAMPIONE, CAMPIONE

Bring on the champions

They went and did it yet again! Manchester United overcame Newcastle's valiant effort to make it three Championships in five years. But who else lifted the silverware at the end of a long, hard season?

Well, it was party time in Sunderland - but can they stay up this time? Swindon bounced back again in Division Two, so their fans had to get used to life at another level once more, and Preston won their first trophy for 25 years when they pipped Gillingham to the Division Three crown.

North of the border, there was more glory for Rangers, this time with Gazza the star of the show, Dunfermline surprisingly held off Dundee United in Division One, while Stirling and new boys Livingston were also top dogs in Scotland.

Check out who won what in our Winner Takes All section...

Champions 1995-96

FA Carling Premiership MANCHESTER UNITED	**GM Vauxhall Conference** STEVENAGE BOROUGH
Endsleigh League Division One SUNDERLAND	**Scottish League Premier Division** RANGERS
Division Two SWINDON TOWN	**First Division** DUNFERMLINE ATHLETIC
Division Three PRESTON NORTH END	**Second Division** STIRLING ALBION
	Third Division LIVINGSTON

Double
UNITED DO IT

MANCHESTER UNITED became the only side in the history of English football to win the League and FA Cup double TWICE when they snatched the Cup in the closing minutes against Liverpool.

Only one player could have broken the deadlock to secure a historic achievement, and Eric Cantona didn't miss his opportunity.

Cantona's winner at Wembley handed Alex Ferguson yet another trophy, his ninth in nine years at the helm.

They include three Premiership titles, two FA Cups, one League Cup, and one European Cup-Winners' Cup. Add to that three runners-up spots in the Premiership, one in the FA Cup and one in the Coca-Cola Cup, and the full picture of Fergie's achievements becomes clear.

He allowed Andrei Kanchelskis, Paul Ince and Mark Hughes to all leave Old Trafford in the summer of 1995, confident that 'The Kids' would be good enough to replace them.

And he was right. David Beckham came in for Kanchelskis, Nicky Butt for Ince, and Paul Scholes shared Mark Hughes' place with Andy Cole.

Add Gary and Phil Neville at the back to that kids' club, and 20-somethings Ryan Giggs and Roy Keane start to look like veterans.

They formed a fantastic attacking ensemble, conducted by Monsieur Cantona. Newcastle thought they'd silenced The Reds but they were unstoppable in the run-in.

Thirteen wins in their last 15 games was the sort of form even Newcastle couldn't cope with and the title headed back to Manchester, shortly followed by the FA Cup.

Ferguson had made history, and no-one could argue with that.

THE KEY MEN

ERIC CANTONA

Footballer of the Year, double-winner, and all-round comeback king. Eric returned from suspension on October 1st 1995, and gave United the sort of massive boost that no-one except Alex Ferguson could have predicted.

His performances were an inspiration to all the youngsters in the United side, and his behaviour was impeccable. But, most importantly to United's double triumph, he scored 19 goals. Four of those came in March when he was United's only League goalscorer, clinching ten vital points along the way.

The script was written for the French superstar to score the winner in the FA Cup Final to win the 'Double, Double' - and his place as an all-time United legend was secured.

Diamonds
AGAIN

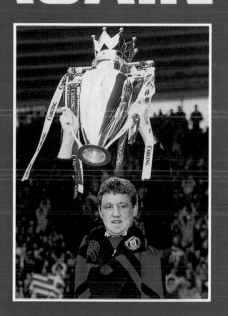

THE CRUNCHERS
THE GAMES THAT WON IT FOR MAN UTD

August 19 ASTON VILLA 3 MAN UNITED 1
With half of the previous season's team absent - sold, injured or suspended in Cantona's case - Fergie fielded 'the kids'. They got stuffed but it taught them a valuable lesson which they never forgot.

October 1 MAN UNITED 2 LIVERPOOL 2
Cantona's comeback, and he scored the late penalty which earned them a point. But Liverpool should have won all three. Two days later, United went out of the Coca-Cola Cup at York.

December 27 MAN UNITED 2 NEWCASTLE 0
Before December, United were right on Newcastle's tail. But three points from five games meant they had to beat Keegan's men. A comfortable win on a freezing night switched the title race back on.

March 4 NEWCASTLE 0 MAN UNITED 1
A 6-0 win at Bolton the week before showed that United were on fire. But this was the big one. The Reds' goal was bombarded by Newcastle but Schmeichel managed to keep everything out. Then Cantona grabbed a goal and closed the gap to one point.

March 16 QPR 1 MAN UNITED 1
United were wobbling in March. Every goal came from Cantona but this was vital. A last gasp equaliser against struggling Rangers put United on top for the first time since September.

April 28 MAN UNITED 5 NOTT'M FOR 0
As Newcastle stumbled, United went for the kill. Having lost at Southampton and struggled to four successive 1-0 wins, this emphatic win all-but sealed the title. All they had to do was avoid defeat at Middlesbrough.

PETER SCHMEICHEL
A massive presence in goal for United, the Danish number one kept his team in so many games during 1995-96 but his importance was only really appreciated when he was absent. Kevin Pilkington is a promising 'keeper but no-one can compare to the great Dane.

His display at Newcastle was one of the greatest ever and sent United on a massive leap towards the title.

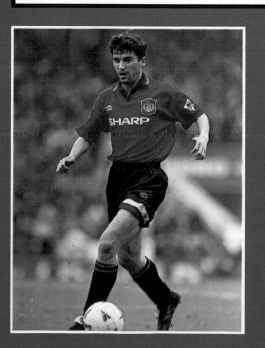

ROY KEANE
Sent off far too often for Fergie's liking, Keane spent large parts of last season suspended. But his aggressive midfield role, when it didn't spill out of order, was a vital component of United's Championship side.

Alongside Nicky Butt, Keane showed Paul Ince would not be missed, and his display in the FA Cup Final, while threatening to get out of control early on, was fantastic.

If he can keep out of trouble, Keane will be a senior member of Mick McCarthy's Republic of Ireland team in their World Cup campaign, despite being only 25-years-old.

And he's Scored!!!!!

Beware - deadly hit men in the area

Goals, goals, goals. There are thousands of them flying in, left, right and centre, and certain gentlemen know how to score them better than others.
Here are those Golden Shoe top League goalscorers in

Alan Shearer

Gary Martindale

Steve White

Premiership
ALAN SHEARER
Blackburn Rovers
31 League Goals in 1995-96
Born: 13 August 1970 in Newcastle
Former Clubs: Southampton
International honours: England Youth, Under-21, B and Full.
* You should know....that Al became the first player to score over 30 League goals in three successive seasons when he scored twice against Wimbledon in his last game of last season.

Second Division
Joint winners
GARY MARTINDALE
Notts County
21 League goals in 1995-96
Born: 24th June

1971 in Liverpool
Former clubs: Bolton, Peterborough
International honours: None
* You should know.....that Gary's older brother Dave was a Tranmere regular for seven years.

MARCUS STEWART
Bristol Rovers

21 League goals in 1995-96
Born: 7th November 1972 in Bristol
Former clubs: None.
International honours: England Under-15s and Football League XI
* You should

Division One
John Aldridge
Tranmere Rovers
27 League goals in 1995-96
Born: 18th September 1958 in Liverpool
Former clubs: Newport, Oxford, Liverpool, Real Sociedad.
International honours: Republic of Ireland full caps.
* You should know...Aldo scored on his last game at Anfield, then threw his boots into the Kop.

know.....Marcus spent two seasons on the bench for England Under-21s without getting on.

Third Division
Joint winners
ANDY SAVILLE
Preston North End
29 League goals in 1995-96
Born: 12th December 1964 in Hull
Former clubs: Hull, Walsall, Barnsley, Hartlepool, Birmingham, Burnley (loan).
International honours: None.
* You should know...that Savo once scored for Hartlepool to end the team's record run of 12 games without a goal!

STEVE WHITE
Hereford United

Andy Saville

Marcus Stewart

29 League goals in 1995-96
Born: 2nd January 1959 in Chipping Sodbury
Former clubs: Bristol Rovers, Luton, Charlton, Lincoln (loan), Swindon.
International honours: None.
* You should know...that Steve has played League football for 20 seasons, but he still started his career in non-League football!

SHOOT/ adidas Golden Shoe
The top League scorers in 1995-96

Premiership
Alan Shearer Blackburn 31
Robbie Fowler Liverpool 28
Les Ferdinand Newcastle 25
Dwight Yorke Aston Villa 17
Teddy Sheringham Tottenham 16
Andrei Kanchelskis Everton 16

Endsleigh League
First Division
John Aldridge Tranmere 27
Doug Freedman C.Palace 23
Paul Barnes Birmingham 22 (15 for York)
Rob Edwards Huddersfield 22 (15 for Crewe)
Dean Sturridge Derby 20
Iwan Roberts Leicester 19
Ian Marshall Ipswich 19

Second Division
Gary Martindale Notts County 21 (15 for Peterborough)
Marcus Stewart Bristol Rovers 21
Kurt Nogan Burnley 20
Shaun Goater Burnley 20
Miguel Desouza Rotherham 18
Karl Connolly Wrexham 18

Third Division
Andy Saville Preston 29
Steve White Hereford 29
Carl Dale Cardiff 21
Steve Whitehall Rochdale 20

Scottish Premier
Pierre Van Hooydonk Celtic
26 League goals in 1995-96
Born: 29th November 1969 in Steenbergen, Holland.
Former clubs: NAC Breda (Holl)
International honours: Holland full caps
* You should know....that Pierre's 1995 Scottish Cup Final goal against Airdrie won Celtic their first trophy for six years.

UP FOR THE

1995-96 THE HONOURS BOARD

FA Cup: Manchester United
Coca-Cola Cup: Aston Villa
Scottish Coca-Cola Cup: Aberdeen
European Cup-Winners' Cup: Paris St Germain
UEFA Cup: Bayern Munich
Auto Windscreens Shield: Rotherham United
Anglo-Italian Cup: Genoa
FA Vase: Brigg Town
Women's FA Cup: Croydon

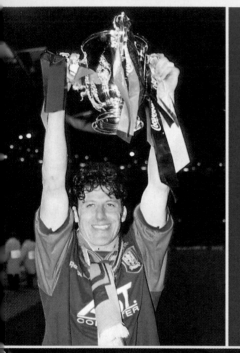

ASTON VILLA 1996 Coca-Cola Cup Winners

Savo Leeds The Way

Villa win Coke at a canter

ASTON VILLA 3 LEEDS 0
(Milosevic 21, Taylor 55, Yorke 89)
Att: 77,056 at Wembley

Goal-den Boys: Yorke, Milosevic and Taylor

That Aston Villa won the Coca-Cola Cup was no great surprise. They were lying fourth in the Premiership when they took on 12th placed Leeds at Wembley in March 1996.

But the way they cruised to a 3-0 win, with Leeds providing little resistance and no attacking spirit whatsoever, shocked even the most loyal Leeds fans.

Savo Milosevic opened the scoring on 21 minutes with an absolute screamer from 30 yards. Ian Taylor made it two with another lovely finish on 55 minutes and Savo put a third on a plate for Dwight Yorke in the last minute. By then, Leeds were destroyed and in utter disarray.

It was a triumph for Villa's delightful attacking football which gave their fans a lot of joy and secured them a place in the UEFA Cup, regardless of their lofty finish in the Premiership.

Carlton Palmer described his team-mates lack of effort in such a major game as "disgraceful" and Leeds could not stop the rot.

They failed to win another game all season, while Villa's relaxed, exciting performances continued right through to May.

CUP!

You won't Sav that! Milosevic sets Villa on the way to Coca-Cola Cup victory

MANCHESTER UNITED 1996 FA Cup Winners

Lovely Doubley

King Cantona does it again

MANCHESTER UNITED 1
LIVERPOOL 0
(Cantona 85)
Att: 79,007 at Wembley

How two of the Premiership's greatest clubs, whose teams played thrilling, top class, football all season, managed to conjure up one of the worst FA Cup Finals of all time, remains a mystery.

But Eric Cantona, the man who had done more than anyone to win the Premiership for Manchester United and get them within reach of a unique double double, put an end to the bore draw with a great, late winner.

The way he took his goal - a controlled volley from David James' underhit punch- - was one of the highlights of the match. Not only did it clinch the Cup and the double, but it was a piece of fantastic skill when the rest of the players looked tired and dispirited, especially Liverpool.

So the Cup went to Old Trafford, and Steve Bruce, left out through injury, persuaded captain for the day Cantona to lift the trophy.

It was a storybook ending to an` incredible season - if only the game had fitted the occassion.

Man-u-fique! Cantona strikes and the Cup is on its way to Old Trafford

And the

THE SECOND ANNUAL FOOTIES was another star-studded affair at Planet Hollywood. Half the Premiership appeared to be there, and the rest of the restaurant was packed out with TV celebs, pop stars and famous faces.

Robbie Fowler's astonishing goals record won him the top prize - SHOOT's Footballer of the Year - voted for by you SHOOT readers out there. Chelsea's teenage sensation Michael Duberry was there to pick up his Young Up and Coming Player Award, Roy Evans picked up the Gaffer of the Year trophy, and the man who attracted every photographer in the land, Mr Ruud Gullit, waltzed up the aisle with style, and gave a classy speech. No surprises there, then!

Taking the Michael... Duberry picks up the Babe Award

More wine please waiter: Roy Evans finds a new job as Deano looks on

Barry Venison with a zebra crossing cunningly disguised as John Barnes

The drink must have been flowing - Dani Behr even found David Baddiel funny!

My name? Oh would you start with the hard ones!

winner is...

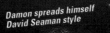
Damon spreads himself David Seaman style

And David Seaman spreads himself Damon style!

Goal King Kinky

GOLDEN BOYS
AND THE WINNERS WERE....
SHOOT Footballer of the Year
ROBBIE FOWLER

Soccerstars Best Young Up and Coming Player **MICHAEL DUBERRY**

90 Minutes Goal of the Year
TONY YEBOAH, Leeds v Liverpool

Goal Gaffer of the Year
ROY EVANS

World Soccer Best International Player in the UK **RUUD GULLIT**

Planet Hollywood Most Entertaining Footballer of the Season
GEORGI KINKLADZE

Sky Sports Mr Nice Guy
JOHN BARNES

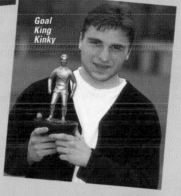
Sweet Sheri - and Teddy as well

Alistair McGowan does his Tony Adams impersonation

WHO WAS THERE?
THE FOOTY STARS; Liverpool: John Barnes, Jason McAteer and Roy Evans **Arsenal:** David Seaman, Scott Marshall and Gavin McGowan **Spurs:** Teddy Sheringham **Aston Villa:** Gareth Southgate and Mark Bosnich **Chelsea:** Ruud Gullit, Michael Duberry and Eddie Newton **QPR:** Andrew Impey and Danny Maddix **Wimbledon:** Dean Holdsworth and Stewart Castledine **Southampton:** Barry Venison and Neil Heaney **Sheffield Wed:** David Pleat **Hearts:** Dave McPherson and John Colquhoun **THE CELEBS:** Damon from Blur, Cindy from EastEnders, PJ and Duncan, Nigel Benn M People's Heather Small, Shaun Edwards, Martin Offiah, Gabrielle, Dani Behr, Ash from Casualty, Ian Astbury from The Cult, Andy Gray off Sky, Sharron Davies and Derek Redmond, Frank Skinner and David Baddiel, Oliver Skeete that dreadlocked show-jumper bloke, Roland Rivron, Shed Seven, Linda Lusardi and the hairdresser from Brookie

Every May, there are tears up and down the country when clubs are going up or going down. Being a football fan can be heart-wrenching. One year you've got a team of heroes scorching up the league, the next, it all goes horribly wrong. Bolton, Luton, Hull and Brighton knew the writing was on the wall last season, but for the likes of Man City, Carlisle, Millwall and Watford, their fate was unknown until virtually the last kick of the season. It's a cruel game.....

Tears and Fears

Up or down, it's an emotional game

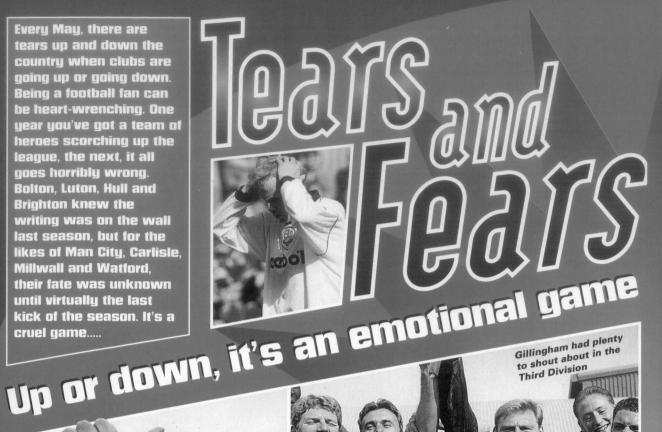

Gillingham had plenty to shout about in the Third Division

The Rams will be raiding the Premiership this season

Going Up, Going Up, Going Up

Sunderland	Bury
Derby	Dunfermline
Swindon	Stirling
Oxford	East Fife
Preston	Livingston
Gillingham	Brechin

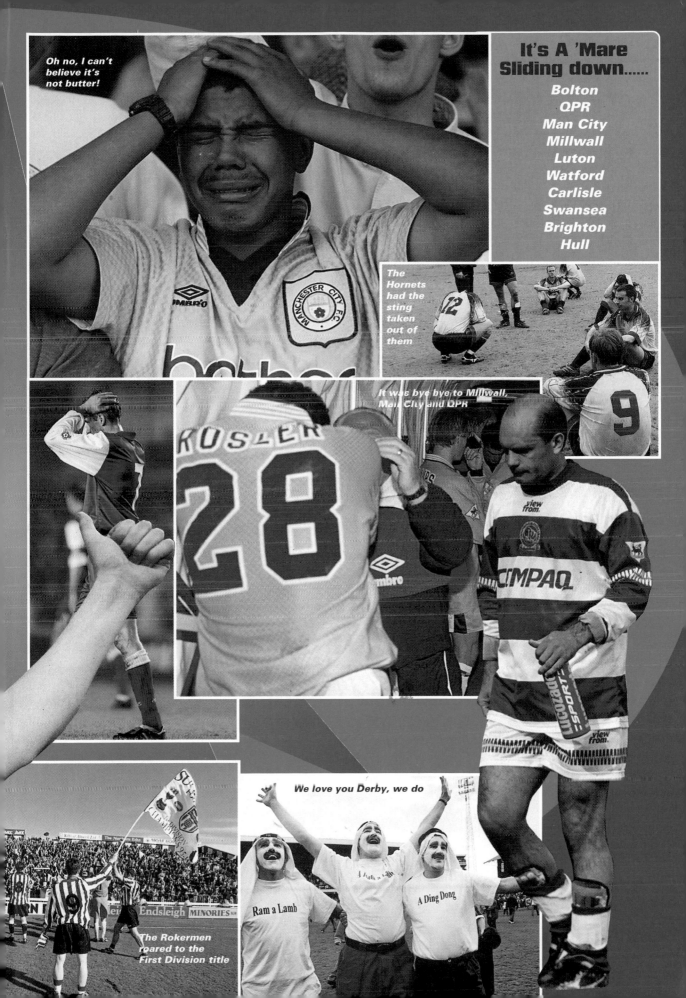

Oh no, I can't believe it's not butter!

It's A 'Mare Sliding down......
Bolton
QPR
Man City
Millwall
Luton
Watford
Carlisle
Swansea
Brighton
Hull

The Hornets had the sting taken out of them

It was bye bye to Millwall, Man City and QPR

We love you Derby, we do

Ram a Lamb

A Ding Dong

The Rokermen roared to the First Division title

KING RICHARD

Richard Gough lifts the Scottish Cup as Rangers complete the double with a 5-1 win over Hearts

GLASGOW

SCOTTISH PREMIER DIVISION CHAMPIONS 1995/6

M RAY ...ONAL METALS MIM

SHOOT ANNUAL 1997 is published by IPC Magazines Ltd., IPC Specialist Group, 24th floor, King's Reach Tower, Stamford Street, London, SE1 9LS. SHOOT ANNUAL must not be sold at more than the recommended selling price shown on the cover. Sole Agents: Australia and New Zealand, Gordon and Gotch Ltd.,; South Africa, Central News Agency Ltd. All rights reserved and reproduction without permission strictly forbidden. Printed in England by BPC Paulton Books Ltd., Paulton, Bristol. Colour origination by Litho Origination, London.

Distributed by Marketforce